WALKING -----➤
SEATTLE

 WILDERNESS PRESS . . . *on the trail since 1967*

WALKING ----→
SEATTLE

35 Tours of the Jet City's Parks, Landmarks, Neighborhoods, and Scenic Views

Second Edition

Clark Humphrey

 WILDERNESS PRESS ... *on the trail since 1967*

Walking Seattle: 35 Tours of the Jet City's Parks, Landmarks, Neighborhoods, and Scenic Views

Second edition, first printing

Copyright © 2018 by Clark Humphrey

Distributed by Publishers Group West
Manufactured in the United States of America

Cover design: Scott McGrew
Cartography: Steve Jones and Scott McGrew; map data: OpenStreetMap
Interior design: Lora Westberg
Cover photo: Gas Works Park © Anthony Ricci/Shutterstock
Interior photos: Clark Humphrey
Frontispiece: The Space Needle (see Walk 7, page 35)

Library of Congress Cataloging-in-Publication Data

Names: Humphrey, Clark, author.
Title: Walking Seattle : 35 tours of the Jet City's parks, landmarks, neighborhoods, and scenic views /
    Clark Humphrey.
Description: Second Edition. | Birmingham, Alabama : Wilderness Press, an imprint of AdventureKEEN,
    [2018] | First edition: 2011. | "Distributed by Publishers Group West"—T.p. verso. | Includes index.
Identifiers: LCCN 2018013227 | ISBN 9780899978130 (paperback) | ISBN 9780899978147 (ebook)
Subjects: LCSH: Walking—Washington (State)—Seattle Metropolitan Area—Guidebooks. | Hiking—
    Washington (State)—Seattle Metropolitan Area—Guidebooks. | Outdoor recreation—Washington
    (State)—Seattle Metropolitan Area—Guidebooks. | Seattle Metropolitan Area (Wash.)—
    Guidebooks.
Classification: LCC GV199.42.W22 S425 2018 | DDC 796.5109797/772—dc23
LC record available at https://lccn.loc.gov/2018013227

Published by 🦫 **WILDERNESS PRESS**
    An imprint of AdventureKEEN
    2204 First Ave. S., Suite 102
    Birmingham, AL 35233
    800-443-7227, fax 205-326-1012

Visit wildernesspress.com for a complete listing of our books and for ordering information. Contact us at our website, at facebook.com/wildernesspress1967, or at twitter.com/wilderness1967 with questions or comments. To find out more about who we are and what we're doing, visit blog.wildernesspress.com.

SAFETY NOTICE: Although Wilderness Press and the author have made every attempt to ensure that the information in this book is accurate at press time, they are not responsible for any loss, damage, injury, or inconvenience that may occur to anyone while using this book. Always check local conditions, know your own limitations, and consult a map.

Acknowledgments

Roslyn Bullas originally hired me to write this book. Gregory Zura first suggested I pursue it.

Many, many people helped me decide what local attractions absolutely had to be included here. A few of them include Revele Kelley, Laura Castellanos, Kurt Geissel, Marlow Harris, Elaine Bonow, Patricia Devine, Julie Pheasant-Albright, Shawn Wolfe, Missy Chow, Bill Shaw, and Mark Harlow.

Author's Note

There's so much to see and do in Seattle. My hardest job was devising only 35 routes that would include most of the city's natural and built attractions. Some of the places that didn't fit are mentioned in sidebars.

Even within the neighborhoods I do cover, space requirements meant I had to leave out a lot of cool places. If you have the time, go ahead and stray from the written path. Just be sure you can retrace your steps.

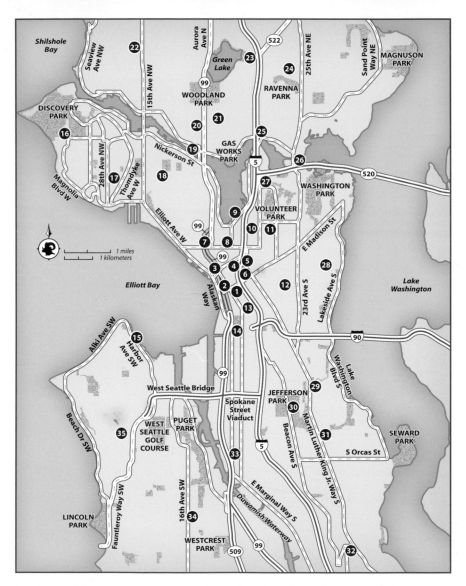

Numbers on this overview map correspond to walk numbers. A map for each tour follows the text for that walk.

Table of Contents

Introduction

This book first came out in the autumn of 2011. What's changed since then? Around here, seemingly almost everything.

Seattle's population, which dipped below 500,000 in the 1980s, is now more than 700,000. Once-quiet commercial streets have become "condo canyons." We are home to two of America's top four retailers and are a center of high-tech trends, from cloud computing to biomedicine.

Waves of affluent, young, mostly male "tech bros" are filling luxury apartments, flooding East Pike Street at night, and turning car traffic into a crowded crawl at all hours.

Fortunately, Seattle is still a great place to walk. And, fortunately, there are still tons of great sights and experiences that you can reach on foot.

Yes, some of the independent stores and restaurants in this book's first edition have left us. But others have emerged. And our many parks, gardens, boulevards, historic landmarks, and spectacular views still beckon.

Our sometimes-steep hills also remain. These walks have been devised to avoid serious inclines. The one exception, in Discovery Park (Walk 16), can be taken in reverse to avoid the steepest climb.

So get on your feet and join me in exploring one of North America's most dynamic, and most beautiful, cities.

1 Pioneer Square
Cobblestones of History

BOUNDARIES: 3rd Ave., Cherry St., 1st Ave. S., and CenturyLink Field
DISTANCE: 1.75 miles
DIFFICULTY: Easy (all flat or downhill)
PARKING: Limited metered street parking; pay lots and garages
PUBLIC TRANSIT: Seattle Transit Tunnel Pioneer Square Station on 3rd Ave., south of Cherry St.;
First Hill Streetcar at S. Jackson St. and Occidental Ave. S.; numerous Metro bus routes on 3rd

The first white settlement in present-day Seattle was established in 1851 at Alki Point (Walk 15). After one miserable winter there, the settlers built a township along a small patch of level land surrounded by forested hills, tidal flats, and Elliott Bay. This is where Henry Yesler built his lumber mill; where the logs for Yesler's mill were skidded downhill on the original Skid Road; where the first stores, saloons, and bawdy houses opened. Those wooden buildings burned in the Great

Seattle Fire of 1889. Brick and stone structures, advertisements of a town striving for greatness, replaced them. These architectural classics were preserved by neglect as downtown's core moved north. They're now mostly intact and restored as monuments to yesterday's hopes for a grand tomorrow.

Walk Description

Start at the ❶ **DoubleTree Arctic Club Hotel,** 700 3rd Ave. Business leaders associated with the Alaska trade built this stoic white-clad structure in 1916. The building notes this connection with rows of terra-cotta walrus heads, whose tusks were originally marble (since replaced with terra-cotta and plastic). The club's meeting space was the grand Dome Room, named for its curved stained glass ceiling. The building is now an elegant boutique hotel; its handsome lounge and dining area are on the floor beneath the Dome Room. Walk southeast from here to Cherry St.

Cross 3rd at Cherry. In front of you is the Dexter Horton Building, another terra-cotta palace. It was built in 1924 for the Dexter Horton National Bank, which merged with two other banks in the 1930s to become Seattle First National Bank (Walk 2). On the southeast side of Cherry stands the Lyon Building, six handsome stories of brick and concrete dating to 1910. Walk on the northwest side of Cherry to 2nd Ave. Across 2nd is the 18-story, Beaux Arts Hoge Building, Seattle's tallest building when it was built in 1911.

Turn left (southeast) on 2nd. Enjoy the terra-cotta angels, serpents, and torches embellishing the Alaska Building. In 1904 it was Seattle's first steel-frame skyscraper (14 stories). Across 2nd is the Broderick Building (623 2nd Ave.), one of the original stone structures built after the 1889 fire. To its left, a parking garage incorporates the ground-floor facade of the 1893 Butler Hotel. Continue on 2nd past three smaller old buildings to ❷ **Smith Tower**.

When typewriter tycoon L. C. Smith built it in 1914, Smith Tower was the tallest building west of the Mississippi. It remained Seattle's tallest until 1962. Its white base is topped by a smaller tower section, and then by a pyramid-shaped cap. The pyramid's base (the building's 35th floor) is the Observatory (formerly the Chinese Room), a lavish space now equipped with a café and bar. The building also features marble-and-brass interiors and Seattle's last old-time steam elevators, with professional operators.

Turn right (west) on Yesler, the original Skid Road, where logs were skidded downhill toward Henry Yesler's sawmill, and continue for two blocks. (Note: Yesler, and the streets south of it, are on a north-south grid. Downtown streets north of Yesler run parallel to the waterfront, on a northwest-southeast grid.) Immediately west of Smith Tower is the infamous "sinking ship" parking garage, built in 1963 on the site of the venerable 1889 Seattle Hotel. A few years later, developers proposed razing most of the neighborhood for more parking. Instead, preservationists had Pioneer Square declared a historic district.

On Yesler's south side are the 1892 Interurban Building and the 1890 ❸ **Merchants Cafe** (still open as a restaurant after 120 years). On its north side, the stoic 1892 Pioneer Building is home to the ❹ **Underground Tour,** founded in the 1980s by entrepreneur-historian Bill Speidel. The guided tour traverses the original ground floors of the square buildings, turned into basements when the street levels were raised.

The Pioneer Building overlooks ❺ **Pioneer Square** itself, also known as Pioneer Place Park. This cobblestoned triangle was established in 1893 on the former site of Yesler's mill. An Alaskan totem pole was added in 1899; it burned, and a new pole was commissioned, in 1938. The ornate iron pergola facing Yesler was built in 1909 (and rebuilt twice since); it was originally a trolley-stop shelter and an entrance to now-closed underground restrooms.

Turn left (south) on 1st Ave. S. In the late 19th and early 20th centuries lumberjacks and farm boys cavorted in saloons and brothels in this great restricted district. In the 1970s this street took on a double life—galleries and boutiques by day, raucous bars by night. Both scenes slumped in the late 2000s but survive, as do the vintage brick buildings. (More recently, a new wave of fancy/costly bistros and bars has come in.) Just south of S. Main St., in the alley between 1st and Alaskan Way, ❻ **Peter Miller Books** is a treasure trove of tomes about architecture, urban history, and design. Toward this segment's end is Sluggers Bar & Grill, which claims to be the first TV-festooned sports bar in the United States.

Turn left (southeast) on the diagonal Railroad Way S. to Occidental Ave. S. You're facing the west side of ❼ **CenturyLink Field,** one of two luxurious stadia that replaced the utilitarian Kingdome. CenturyLink hosts the National Football League's Seahawks, Major League Soccer's Sounders FC, concerts, and boat and home shows.

Turn left (north) on Occidental, abutting CenturyLink Field's parking lot. To your left is the Florentine (526 1st Ave. S.), a condo and retail structure built from a really long 1909 warehouse. Occidental doglegs at S. King St. in front of the former site of F. X. McRory's, which had been a luxurious sports bar dating from the humbler Kingdome era.

Turn right (east) on S. King. To your right loom several new residential high-rises. One of them houses ❽ **13 Coins,** the city's premier 24-hour fine-dining eatery (recently moved from South Lake Union). Behind these buildings lies CenturyLink Field's north entrance, featuring artist Bob Haozous's *Earth Dialogue,* four disk-shaped silhouettes representing humanity's connection to the natural world. Ahead of you lies ❾ **King Street Station,** built in 1906. Its 242-foot clock tower was

CenturyLink Field in front of Mount Rainier

inspired by Venice's Campanile di San Marco. It now services Amtrak and commuter rail. Its grand waiting room, once turned ugly by a 1960s modernization, has now been elegantly restored.

Turn left (north) from King onto 2nd Ave. S. To your right, a new King County office building strives to fit in with its historic surroundings. To your left, the Court in the Square is a glass-ceilinged atrium between two brick buildings.

Turn left (west) onto S. Jackson St. To your right, the historic Cadillac Hotel now houses the ❿ **Klondike Gold Rush National Historical Park,** a free museum about the 1897 Yukon gold fever that helped put Seattle on the map. To your left, Zeitgeist Coffee is a handsome, retro-industrial space. Beyond it stands the 1903 Washington Shoe Building, a factory that later became art studios and now hosts offices.

Turn right and walk north through Occidental Mall. This pedestrian-only corridor abuts several fine art galleries and serves as a more intimate counterpart to ⓫ **Occidental Park,** the next block north. The latter features two large totem poles and the *Fallen Firefighter Memorial* statues.

Turn right (east) on S. Main St., past the sleek new headquarters of Weyerhaeuser (the vastly downsized timber giant). At the southeast corner of 2nd and Main, the 1929 Seattle Fire Department headquarters stands as a stony symbol of stoic dedication. At the northwest corner of 2nd and Main, the ⓬ **Waterfall Garden Park** is a small enclosed outdoor space in front of an artificial waterfall. The family who founded the formerly Seattle-based United Parcel Service built it in 1977. Farther along, Main Street Gyros occupies a vintage gas station at the intersection with the diagonal 2nd Ave. Extension. The northeast corner of 3rd and Main offers more major commercial art galleries.

Turn left (north) on 3rd Ave. S. Dorothea "Lou" Graham, early Seattle's most famous brothel operator, originally commissioned the 1890 Washington Court Building at the southwest corner

Backstory: Seattle's Street System

Seattle's street-naming system is really easy once you know the basic rules (which have their exceptions). Streets generally run east–west; in greater downtown (including Belltown and west Capitol Hill), they run northeast–southwest. Avenues generally run north–south; in greater downtown, they run northwest–southeast. Ways, drives, places, boulevards, and so on can run in any direction.

Downtown isn't the only place where the city's geography inspired digressions from an orderly street grid. Just about every part of town has them.

These walks routinely cross the city's directional prefix and suffix zones (NW, N, NE, and so on). Don't worry about it.

Central downtown's streets were given alliterative pairs of names for easier remembering—Jefferson and James, Columbia and Cherry, Marion and Madison, Spring and Seneca, University and Union, and Pike and Pine. These are expressed in an old-time local phrase, "Jesus Christ Made Seattle Under Protest."

of 3rd and Washington. It's now part of the Union Gospel Mission. At the northeast corner, the Tashiro/Kaplan Building combines two vintage structures into artist studios and galleries.

Turn left (west) on S. Washington St. and go five blocks. At the northeast corner of Washington and the 2nd Ave. Extension, the three-story 1890 Chin Gee Hee Building is the last vestige of Seattle's original Chinatown, before that community gradually moved farther east (Walk 13). At this intersection's northwest corner, the Nugent/Considine Block housed the Double Header Tavern, Seattle's oldest gay bar until its 2015 closing. The space is now Nightjar (from the current owners of Re-bar [Walk 8]) and contains framed images of its Double Header legacy. In that building's basement, the Stage Seattle nightclub occupies vaudeville mogul John Considine's People's Theater. One block beyond was the 1950s brutalism of the Alaskan Way Viaduct (Walk 3), which may have been razed by the time you read this. At the foot of Alaskan Way stands the Washington Street Boat Landing, a Beaux Arts metal pergola built in 1920.

Turn right (northwest) on Alaskan. After one block turn right (east) on Yesler. The 1914 Pioneer Square Hotel and Saloon has been renovated as a boutique hotel. Back at 1st and Yesler, the red sandstone facade of the Mutual Life Building has been home to ⓭ **Magic Mouse Toys,** which offers toys from around the world, since 1977.

This walk starts one block southwest of Walk 4, and it ends near Walks 2 and 3. At Railroad and Occidental you're one block north of Walk 14. At 2nd and Jackson you're three blocks west and one block north of Walk 13.

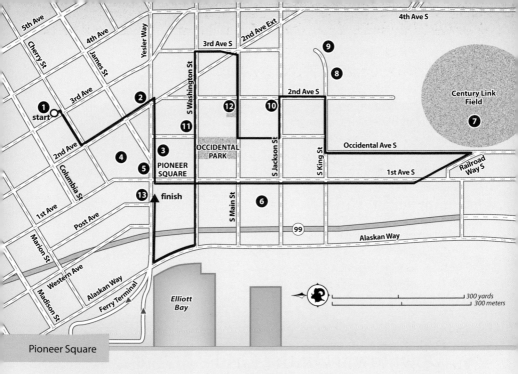

Points of Interest

① **DoubleTree Arctic Club Hotel** 700 3rd Ave., 206-340-0340, thearcticclubseattle.com

② **Smith Tower** 506 2nd Ave., 206-624-0414, smithtower.com

③ **Merchants Cafe and Saloon** 109 Yesler Way, 206-467-5070, merchantscafeandsaloon.com

④ **Bill Speidel's Underground Tour** 614 1st Ave., 206-682-4646, undergroundtour.com

⑤ **Pioneer Square** 1st Ave. and Yesler Way, seattle.gov/parks/find/parks/pioneer-square

⑥ **Peter Miller Books** 304 Alaskan Way S. (entrance in Post Alley), 206-441-4114, petermiller.com

⑦ **CenturyLink Field** 800 Occidental Ave. S., 206-381-7555, centurylinkfield.com

⑧ **13 Coins** 255 S. King St., 206-682-2513, 13coins.com

⑨ **King Street Station** 303 S. Jackson St., 206-398-5000, seattle.gov/transportation/kingstreet.htm

⑩ **Klondike Gold Rush National Historical Park** 319 2nd Ave. S., 206-220-4240, nps.gov/klse

⑪ **Occidental Park** Occidental Ave. S. and S. Washington St., seattle.gov/parks/find/parks/occidental-square

⑫ **Waterfall Garden Park** 219 2nd Ave. S., pioneersquare.org/experiences/waterfall-garden-park

⑬ **Magic Mouse Toys** 603 1st Ave., 206-682-8097, magicmousetoys.com

2 Downtown: Off the Grid
Taking the Shortcut

BOUNDARIES: Western Ave., Union St., Freeway Park, Alaskan Way, and Marion St.
DISTANCE: 1.5 miles
DIFFICULTY: Moderate (a few mild inclines)
PARKING: Limited metered street parking; pay lots and garages, including a lot at Western and University and a garage at Western and Seneca St.
PUBLIC TRANSIT: Metro routes 10, 47, and 99 stop at 1st Ave. and University St.; Seattle Transit Tunnel University Street Station at 2nd and University

Downtown's spectacular vistas come with a price. Parts of it are almost too steep to walk. (Some side-street sidewalks are equipped with raised concrete ridges, to help prevent pedestrians from falling backward. Really.) Fortunately, there are ways to lessen this burden. City zoning has long encouraged property owners to add elevators, escalators, tunnels, and other amenities to help move people around the hardest hill climbs. All the shortcuts in this walk (including those on private property) are open to the public, at least during business hours. They also offer up-close and inside views of some of the city's most spectacular artificial spectacles, from Freeway Park's giant flower box setting to Seattle Tower's understated elegance to the Exchange Building's Deco glamour.

Walk Description

Start at Western Ave. and University St. A century ago, Western was the Commission District, home to Seattle's wholesale produce industry. Now its warehouses are loft offices. A whale mural by James Crespinel stands at the northwest corner of this intersection, on the Seattle Steam Co. plant (an independent central-heating provider). To your right are the **❶ Harbor Steps,** a grand outdoor stairway straddling an office, condo, hotel, and retail complex. Climb these steps, or take the public elevator just south of University, to 1st Ave.

Cross 1st at University's north side to the original (1991) end of the **❷ Seattle Art Museum,** which architect Robert Venturi intended to resemble an upmarket version of a decorated shed, albeit a shed clad in limestone and granite. Take the wide outdoor plaza steps to 2nd Ave. and cross.

Pay your respects to the region's war dead at the Garden of Remembrance, on the 2nd Ave. side of Benaroya Hall near a transit tunnel entrance. Cross University to the northern entrance of the 1201 Third Avenue Building (formerly Washington Mutual Tower, the older of two towers built for that defunct bank). Take the escalator to, then exit through, the 3rd Ave. lobby.

Cross 3rd and enter the **❸ Seattle Tower** lobby, an Art Deco dreamscape in bronze and marble. Take the elevators to the fifth floor. There, take a right and leave through the alley skybridge to the plaza outside the Financial Center building. Descend that plaza's outdoor stairs.

Cross kitty-corner at 4th and University, taking a gander at the Olympic Hotel and Cobb Building (Walk 4) and the **❹ Rainier Square** tower, with its unique tapered concrete base. (It will soon be shadowed by a much larger tower on the block's north half.)

Cross 5th to the 5th Avenue Theater's entrance. At its right, you'll find stairs down to a pedestrian concourse. This three-block-long underground passage connects to the Skinner Building, Seattle Hilton, and Washington Athletic Club. Its walls are lined with big posters chronicling the history of downtown Seattle and that of Seattle's onetime biggest employer, the Boeing Company.

This concourse ends at a pair of escalators. Take the up escalator into Two Union Square's food court. Walk toward a small waiting area with a fireplace. Turn left. At your earliest opportunity, turn right. Take a shorter escalator up, into the building's upper lobby level. Walk straight and out the building, onto another skybridge.

On this skybridge, look left and admire the stately old Eagles Auditorium, now home to **❺ ACT (A Contemporary Theatre).** It hosted acid-rock acts in the 1960s; despite popular legend,

Jimi Hendrix never played there. Turn right and enter the Washington State Convention Center's second floor. Rotating public art exhibits line its corridors.

Take an escalator jaunt to the Convention Center's fourth floor. Walk straight from the escalator's end toward a big glass wall. Take the glass doors to your left, out of the Convention Center and into ❻ **Freeway Park.** This labyrinth of landscaped concrete platforms predates the Convention Center by a decade. When I-5 was routed between downtown and First Hill in the early 1960s, some residents protested. They called for a roof over the freeway to keep the two neighborhoods connected. They got a small lid years later, in 1976.

Walk straight ahead through Freeway Park. At the first path intersection, take a right-and-left dogleg. At the next intersection, take a hard right. Walk downhill to the park's tail end at the outdoor plaza of the Park Place tower, at 6th Ave. and Seneca St.

Cross kitty-corner at 6th and Seneca. At this intersection's northwest corner stands ❼ **Plymouth Church Seattle,** a stunning example of a modern Protestant church, all white and asymmetrical. At the southwest corner, the Crowne Plaza Hotel's developers promised a public open space in return for getting to build a taller hotel. They built a tiny windswept plaza atop a very obscure flight of stairs (just try to find it). Go southeast on 6th one block to the University Women's Club, a brick Georgian Revival building.

Seattle Tower

Turn southwest on Spring St., passing the Nakamura Courthouse. Turn southeast on 5th to the ❽ **Seattle Central Library,** a postmodern masterwork opened in 2004 and designed by Dutch architect Rem Koolhaas. Its asymmetric stacks allow different square footage for different uses, leading to a spectacular reading room on the 10th floor. Enter at the library's southeast side. Take the escalator down to the first floor; exit the library at 4th Ave.

Cross 4th at Madison St. to ❾ **Safeco Plaza.** This 50-story black box was Seattle's tallest building when built in 1968 (downtown's first big privately funded building in nearly 40 years). It opened as the headquarters of Seattle-First

Backstory: The WTO

In their eternal obsession with being seen as a world-class city, Seattle's civic leaders successfully lobbied to host the World Trade Organization's 1999 ministerial conference. Despite the presence of many 1960s generation vets in the city council and other official bodies, nobody seemed to think mass protests could occur against the WTO; even though it was widely reviled for, among other things, ordering national governments to change their laws to appease corporations.

On what the protesters called N30 (November 30, 1999), more than 40,000 demonstrators took to the downtown streets, blocking Convention Center access. A smaller team of black-clothed anarchists, meanwhile, spray-painted and threw rocks at chain store windows. Police used pepper spray, tear gas, and rubber bullets to force the demonstrators out of the immediate area. The daylong Battle in Seattle was later fictionalized in a movie of the same name—mostly filmed in Vancouver, British Columbia.

National Bank, the state's largest bank until it decided to speculate in Oklahoma oil leases in the 1980s. Seafirst was sold to Bank of America for pennies on the dollar. The building is now headquarters to a homegrown insurance company, itself sold to Liberty Mutual. Pass Henry Moore's *Vertebrae* sculpture, enter the main lobby, take the elevators or escalators down, and exit onto 3rd Ave.

Cross kitty-corner at 3rd and Madison. Walk through the lobby of the trapezoidal Wells Fargo Center. At its western end, take a covered outdoor escalator down to 2nd and Marion St.

Cross kitty-corner at 2nd and Marion, passing the Henry M. Jackson Federal Building (with the entry arch and other pieces of the stone midrise it replaced, the Burke Building, now used as plaza art). At this intersection's southwest corner, the 1929 Exchange Building is another Art Deco masterpiece. Enter its dark marble lobby with a gilt ceiling; take its elevators to, and exit through, its 1st Ave. level.

Cross 1st at Marion to the Colman Building. This block-long midrise was built in stages between 1889 and 1904, and has been remodeled several times since. Walk one block southwest on Marion back to Western and turn right. You'll soon pass the ❿ **Center for Architecture & Design,** with exhibits and displays about the city's "built" past and future. Or you can take a skybridge at the Colman Building's north side to the Washington State Ferry Terminal.

This walk connects easily to four other walks. It crosses Walk 4 at several points and crosses Walk 3 at 1st Ave. At 1st and Marion you're three blocks northwest of Walk 1. At 6th and Seneca you're two blocks southeast of Walk 6.

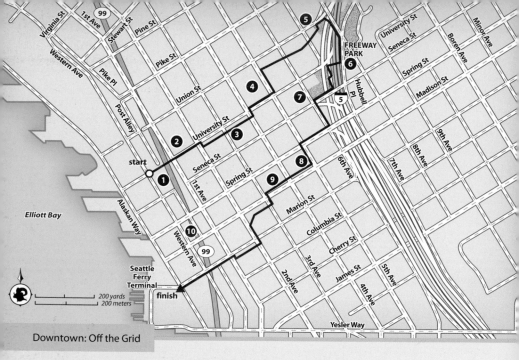

Points of Interest

1. **Harbor Steps** Western Ave. and University St.
2. **Seattle Art Museum** 1300 1st Ave., 206-654-3100, seattleartmuseum.org
3. **Seattle Tower** 1218 3rd Ave.
4. **Rainier Square** 4th Ave. and University St., rainiersquare.com
5. **ACT** 700 Union St., 206-292-7676, acttheatre.org
6. **Freeway Park** 700 Seneca St., seattle.gov/parks/find/parks/freeway-park
7. **Plymouth Church Seattle** 1217 6th Ave., 206-622-4865, plymouthchurchseattle.org
8. **Seattle Central Library** 1000 4th Ave., 206-386-4636, spl.org
9. **Safeco Plaza** 1001 4th Ave., safeco.com
10. **Center for Architecture & Design** 1010 Western Ave., 206-667-9184, cfadseattle.org

3 Pike Place Market, 1st Ave., and the Waterfront Fish, Fruit, and Fun

BOUNDARIES: 1st Ave., Virginia St., 15th Ave. W., and W. Howe St.
DISTANCE: 5.5 miles, in 3 segments
DIFFICULTY: Moderate (1 short incline)
PARKING: Limited metered street parking; pay lots and garages include the Pike Place Market garage at Western Ave. and Pine St.
PUBLIC TRANSIT: Many Metro routes stop at 3rd Ave. and Virginia St. The Transit Tunnel's Westlake Station has an exit at 3rd Ave. and Pine St.

For more than 110 years, Pike Place has been home to the oldest continuously operating farmers' market in the United States. It's a fascinating concoction of produce, flowers, crafts, antiques, magic, and more, hugging a bluff looming over the central waterfront on Elliott Bay. The waterfront's docks and freight sheds have been reinvented for tourism, recreation, and pleasure travel. Myrtle Edwards Park and Olympic Sculpture Park have given the area two collective front lawns.

Currently, the waterfront is undergoing a multiyear makeover. A new seawall is being built, and a new wide surface street and park boulevard are in the works.

Hint: To get the most out of this walk, avoid the market's peak tourist days (especially summer Saturdays).

Walk Description

Start at 1st Ave., heading southeast from Virginia St. At this intersection's southeast corner, the 11-story Terminal Sales Building was built in 1923 as showrooms for manufacturers and wholesalers. Now it has high-ceilinged loft offices. At its southwest corner, the century-old ❶ **Virginia Inn** bar and bistro denotes the start of the Pike Place Market Historic District.

Continue along 1st for three blocks, past colorful places to shop (including ❷ **Metsker Maps**) and eat (Le Pichet, Shug's Soda Fountain, and El Borracho). Just before Pike, take in the brassy animated sign for the Déjà Vu strip club, a remnant of 1st Ave.'s grittier former character. Up Pike between 1st and 2nd is a big neon guitar above a Hard Rock Cafe. But the sign you're looking for is to your right on Pike. It's the historic PUBLIC MARKET CENTER sign with its proudly analog neon clock. Take a right into the ❸ **Pike Place Market.** Then immediately take another right into the Corner Market Building's lower arcade level, past the ❹ **Can Can** cabaret.

Go northwest through the Corner Market and the adjacent Sanitary Public Market building, past ethnic food stands, a meat market, a dairy store, and more. At this corridor's northern end take a left to enter Post Alley, an outdoor promenade offering more snacking and shopping.

Head right (northwest) on Post Alley for three blocks. You find restaurants and bars of many types and price points (including the Irish-style Kells and the Italian-style Pink Door), a tearoom, and a boutique hotel. You end up back at Virginia.

Go left (southwest) on Virginia to the northwest side of Pike Place; take another left. Stroll along the market's main drag back to Pike St. Along your way are hundreds of tourists, depending on the season, plus Indian, Mexican, and Filipino groceries; sausage and *hum bow* stands; the historic Three Girls bakery and sandwich counter; and what's billed as the world's first Starbucks. (The real first Starbucks was in a now-razed building a block away.)

When you get back to the L-shaped intersection of Pike Place and Pike St., hang a right. You're now facing the market's Main Arcade, under the clock. Two of the market's most-photographed attractions are here—Rachel, the full-size piggy bank (proceeds from her coin slot benefit services for downtown seniors and low-income residents), and the Pike Place Fish Co., with its high-energy staffers tossing fish. Before you enter this section, look up to view five paintings by Aki Sogabe commemorating the Japanese American farmers who sold produce here before they were sent to relocation camps during World War II.

Take a right to walk northwest along the Main Arcade. Besides more tourists, you spot the market's original raison d'être, the low stall and high stall produce stands. (The former are farmer run; the latter are year-round retail ventures.) You also see two popular-price restaurant bars with spectacular waterfront views (the Athenian and Lowell's), a closet-sized souvenir store, and another fish market (Pure Food Fish). The Main Arcade directly leads into the North Arcade, a long line of tables with artists and craftspeople. A short skybridge leads to MarketFront, a new set of stalls and shops plus an outdoor plaza, all built atop a new parking garage.

One of Pike Place's several fish markets

Turn around at the North Arcade's end, and backtrack past the craft sellers until you reach the Main Arcade's northwestern end. You see a ramp to the Down Under shops. Descend into a plank-floored indoor corridor of shops selling magic supplies, posters, postcards, beads, health food, candy, comic books, vintage clothing, and more.

The southern end of the Down Under Arcade leads to exterior doors, which lead to the Pike Street Hill Climb, an elevator and series of outdoor stairs leading six stories from the Market's main level down to the waterfront. Take the stairs or elevator back to the south end of the Main Arcade. When you near Rachel the Pig, take a right-left dogleg into the Economy Market, a short series of stands and storefronts paralleling the end of Pike St. Its attractions include a magazine stand, a mini-donut stand, and an Italian deli and wine shop.

Along the Economy Market's south wall, find a signed passageway leading to the Economy Market Atrium. Take a right and go through the atrium, a two-story indoor agora with shops selling wind-up toys, herbal supplements, and modern art made by local American Indians. Its upper level leads to Folio: The Seattle Athenaeum, a private library and literary center. This room's southern end has a doorway marked TO MORE SHOPS AND RESTAURANTS. Take it into the indoor corridor of the South Arcade, a new building anchored by the Pike Pub and Brewery. It leads to 1st Ave. and Union St.

Return to 1st. To your left, the ❺ **Showbox at the Market** is a vintage big-band ballroom and one of Seattle's premier music venues. Take a right across Union and walk southeast along 1st. Where sailors and dockworkers once downed beers and watched pornos now stand galleries, bistros, a Four Seasons Hotel, and the ❻ **Seattle Art Museum**. (The latter occupies the lower levels of the Russell Investments Center, formerly WaMu Center, the second tower built by the now-defunct Washington Mutual Bank.)

At 1st and University, ❼ **Von's 1000 Spirits** is a fancy burger-and-seafood restaurant with many liquors from local microdistilleries. Three blocks down at Madison, the Kimpton Alexis Hotel houses the Bookstore Bar + Café. Across Madison, the Old Federal Office Building is a brick-and-aluminum Art Deco treasure, a fine complement to the Colman Building one block away at Marion St. (Walk 2). At Cherry St., the 1903 Lowman Building has a French Renaissance–inspired gabled roofline. That building abuts Pioneer Square, which takes you two more blocks to S. Washington St. and the end of our first segment. You can stop now by taking a bus at 3rd and Washington back to Pike St.

If you're still with us, turn right (west) on Washington to the Public Boat Landing, Alaskan Way and S. Washington St. This ornate wrought-iron pergola is the perfect gateway from Pioneer Square (rock-solid yet frilly) to the waterfront (all wood, creosote, and water). To the east, the 1950s concrete brutalism of the Alaskan Way Viaduct is gone or soon will be when you read this.

In getting here, you've probably crossed the Waterfront Streetcar tracks. From 1982 to 2005, refurbished 1930s trolleys from Melbourne, Australia, rolled along Alaskan Way, through Pioneer Square, and to the International District. They were mothballed when their garage was razed as part of the Olympic Sculpture Park. Parts of the tracks have since been removed or paved over.

Walk northwest along the west side of Alaskan Way. Originally a wooden rail trestle over the water, it was filled in and paved in the early 20th century. Here's what you'll find, pier by pier (don't worry about numbers jumping ahead; some piers were razed or consolidated):

Seattle Great Wheel and a Washington State Ferry

Pier 50: The ❽ **King County Water Taxi** runs a passenger ferry service to Alki (Walk 15).

Pier 52: The main ❾ **Washington State Ferry Terminal**, with car and passenger service to Bremerton and Bainbridge Island, is part of the world's third-largest ferry network.

Pier 53: Fire Station 5 is home to the city's fireboat fleet.

Pier 54: This first of five classic woodshed piers hosts ❿ **Ivar's Acres of Clams**, the waterfront's anchor restaurant since 1938, when radio personality Ivar Haglund started a private aquarium and roadside fish stand. It now offers indoor dining, plus an outdoor fish bar with bench seating under heat lamps. Also on Pier 54 is Ye Olde Curiosity Shop, a gift and novelty store (and home to a glass-encased mummy named Sylvester).

Pier 55: Red Robin, the formerly Seattle-based burger chain, has a branch here. Outside, ⓫ **Argosy Cruises'** nine boats offer sightseeing, dining, and party cruises around the sound.

Pier 56: Another Argosy dock abuts Elliott's Oyster House.

Pier 57: Outside, the 175-foot-tall ⓬ **Seattle Great Wheel** is one of those giant Ferris wheels that have popped up in cities around the world. Inside, a wooden carousel and a virtual-reality Washington travelogue "ride" lie behind a restaurant and an import shop.

Pier 58: Waterfront Park is a concrete open space, seldom used for anything these days. (Across from here are the Highway 99 Blues Club and the Seattle Antiques Market.)

Pier 59: The ⓭ **Seattle Aquarium** features local and exotic sea critters in 400,000 gallons of water. Across, at Alaskan and Pike, is the Pike Street Hill Climb, a staircase and elevator up to the Pike Place Market and downtown. It will be revamped and enlarged as part of the ongoing waterfront makeover in 2019–2020. You can take the Hill Climb back to the market or continue on Alaskan.

Piers 62–63: A now-razed wood-planked open space used to host summer concerts. Across Alaskan, condos and a hotel squeeze into a narrow strip of land between Alaskan, the Viaduct, and the railroad tracks.

Piers 64–66: The ⓮ **Bell Street Pier** complex replaced three old woodshed piers in the 1990s. It includes a small-boat marina, a seafood restaurant, a now-closed maritime museum, a conference center, a cruise-ship terminal, and a pedestrian skybridge to Belltown (Walk 7). Across Alaskan stands part of the Art Institute of Seattle.

Pier 67: The ⓯ **Edgewater Hotel** is Seattle's only on-the-water hostelry. Once *the* local place to stay for touring rock bands (and their female admirers, as noted in the Frank Zappa song "Mudshark"), it's now gussied up with ski-lodge trappings and a water-view restaurant.

Pier 69: The ⓰ *Victoria Clipper's* day trips to Victoria, B.C. (and seasonally to other places, such as the Skagit Valley Tulip Festival), depart here.

Pier 70: A 1902 fish-packing warehouse became a minimall and disco in 1972. In 1998 it was the main setting for MTV's *The Real World*. It now houses law offices and an upscale restaurant.

At Pier 70, Alaskan Way turns into the northeast-heading Broad St. Take a right onto Broad and go two uphill blocks to Western Ave.; turn left into the ⓱ **Olympic Sculpture Park's** main entrance. The privately funded outdoor exhibit space (on the former Union 76 petroleum storage depot) is a nine-acre blend of lawns, trails, gardens, an indoor nature exhibit, and more than a dozen medium-to-huge, abstract-to-postmodern metal monuments.

Take the Sculpture Park's 2,200-foot main path as it zigzags back to the waterfront, at the southern end of Myrtle Edwards Park. The walk's second segment ends here. You can take a 99 bus (weekdays only) at Elliott Ave. and Broad back to your start or continue with segment three.

Still with us? Then take a right into ⓲ **Myrtle Edwards Park** and follow its main trail heading northwest. This trail hugs the shoreline for 1.2 miles, starting with a short artificial beach that is part of the Sculpture Park. From there it's paved trails, rocky shore, grass, and trees (and fenced-off freight tracks to your right).

Sights along your way through the park include the P-I Globe (a 30-foot steel-and-neon sign that advertised the sadly missed *Post-Intelligencer* newspaper and still promotes its spinoff website), a small lighthouse statue (memorializing fishermen who died at sea), a rose garden, a fishing pier, and a pedestrian bridge with double-helix design features (leading to what was a biotech corporate campus but now houses Expedia). At one point the path goes under a conveyor crane to a grain terminal.

At the park's northern end, the trail bends north as the Terminal 91 Bike Path, maintained by the Port of Seattle. It parallels the Smith Cove Waterway, one of the Pacific Coast's largest vehicle import terminals. If you're lucky, you can spot Japan's latest models being driven off freighter ships. Take this trail up to the Magnolia Bridge.

Follow the signs onto the Magnolia Bridge's pedestrian lane and head right (east) over the railroad tracks, to 15th Ave. W. and W. Garfield St.

Turn left (north) and walk two blocks to a strip mall at 15th and W. Newton St. Or turn south and walk two blocks to Champion Party Supply (a year-round Halloween party headquarters). Or take a 19, 24, 32, 33, or RapidRide D bus at 15th and Garfield back to Virginia St.

This walk connects easily to six other walks. It crosses Walk 2 at 1st and University. Its start crosses Walk 7. It crosses Walk 1 at Yesler Way. At 1st and Pine you're two blocks southwest of Walk 4. At Pier 50 you're at the start of Walk 15. At Western and Broad you're seven blocks south of Walk 18.

Points of Interest

① **Virginia Inn** 1937 1st Ave., 206-728-1937, virginiainnseattle.com

② **Metsker Maps** 1511 1st Ave., 206-623-8747, metskers.com

③ **Pike Place Market** 1st Ave. and Pike St., 206-682-7453, pikeplacemarket.org

④ **Can Can** 94 Pike St., 206-652-0832, thecancan.com

⑤ **Showbox at the Market** 1426 1st Ave., 206-628-3151, showboxonline.com

Pike Place Market, 1st Ave., and the Waterfront

6 **Seattle Art Museum** 1300 1st Ave., 206-654-3100, seattleartmuseum.org

7 **Von's 1000 Spirits** 1225 1st Ave., 206-621-8667, vons1000spirits.com

8 **King County Water Taxi** Alaskan Way and Yesler Way, Pier 50, 206-477-3979, kingcounty.gov/depts /transportation/water-taxi/vashon

9 **Washington State Ferry Terminal** 801 Alaskan Way, Pier 52, 206-464-6400, wsdot.wa.gov/ferries

10 **Ivar's Acres of Clams** 1001 Alaskan Way, Pier 54, 206-624-6852, ivars.com

11 **Argosy Cruises** 1101 Alaskan Way, Piers 55–56, 206-623-1445, argosycruises.com

12 **Seattle Great Wheel** 1301 Alaskan Way, Pier 57, 206-623-8607, seattlegreatwheel.com

13 **Seattle Aquarium** 1483 Alaskan Way, Pier 59, 206-386-4300, seattleaquarium.org

14 **Bell Street Pier** 2203 Alaskan Way, Pier 66, 206-787-3911, tinyurl.com/bellstpier

15 **Edgewater Hotel** 2411 Alaskan Way, Pier 67, 206-728-7000, edgewaterhotel.com

16 *Victoria Clipper* 2701 Alaskan Way, Pier 69, 206-448-5000, clippervacations.com

17 **Olympic Sculpture Park** 2901 Western Ave., 206-654-3100, seattleartmuseum.org

18 **Myrtle Edwards Park** 3130 Alaskan Way W., 206-684-4075, seattle.gov/parks/find/parks /myrtle-edwards-park

4 Downtown: The Retail Core and Financial District Commerce and Culture

BOUNDARIES: 9th Ave., Pine St., 3rd Ave., and James St.
DISTANCE: 2 miles
DIFFICULTY: Moderate (1 uphill block)
PARKING: Limited metered street parking; pay lots and garages include Pacific Place Garage (6th Ave. north of Pine St.)
PUBLIC TRANSIT: Seattle Transit Tunnel Westlake Station at 5th Ave. and Pine St.; Metro routes 10, 11, 43, 47, and 49 serve Pike and Pine Sts.

Seattle is blessed to have an active, dynamic downtown that never succumbed to the urban decay faced by other cities around the United States. It might not be a 24-hour place, but it's at least a 16-hour place. And it's devoted to more than the mere making and spending of money. It offers a wide range of live and filmed entertainments. It has a major art museum and many private galleries. It has occasional peekaboo views of the Elliott Bay waterfront and the Olympic

Mountains. And as you're about to see, it sports an array of architectural styles, from 1920s Art Deco whimsy to postmodern color play and angularity.

Walk Description

Start at the ❶ **Paramount Theater,** on the southeast corner of 9th Ave. and Pine St. Seattle's master theater designer B. Marcus Priteca helped create this sumptuous 1928 film-and-vaudeville palace, with a handsome brick exterior and a Versailles-inspired interior. The blue vertical sign outside is a 2009 copy of the original. Looking northwest on 9th, you can see the rooftop Gothic neon announcing the 1926-built Camlin Hotel, now part of a time-share circuit.

Go left (southwest) on Pine. At the southeast corner of 8th and Pine, the cylindrical Tower 801 apartment building houses a retro-modern Caffe Ladro at its base. Kitty-corner from there, the Paramount Hotel's Dragonfish bar offers happy-hour sushi bites.

Cross Pine at the southeast corner with 7th Ave. toward the ❷ **Pacific Place** mall. Opened in 1998, it's a single full-block building disguised with a variety of false facades. Within, upscale chain stores and a multiplex cinema surround a four-story atrium. Across 6th, the Nordstrom flagship store and headquarters building (a handsome white 1918 structure) was remodeled in 1998 from the former Frederick & Nelson, a classy (and still missed) department store that folded in 1992.

On the next block, the ❸ **Westlake Center** mall and office tower was built a decade before Pacific Place, when Seattle's business leaders were less obsessed with high-end luxury everything. Westlake Center has Nordstrom's Rack outlet store and a Taco del Mar burrito stand; Pacific Place has Tiffany's and the Italian-bistro chain Il Fornaio. (Westlake has also done some upscaling of its own and now houses Zara and Saks Off Fifth.) Across Pine from Westlake Center, triangular Westlake Park is the site of high-profile political rallies and commercial publicity events.

At the northwest side of 4th is Seattle's other heritage department store, built in 1928 as The Bon Marché. It now bears the Macy's brand, but old-timers still call it the Bon. Like the Frederick & Nelson (now Nordstrom) building, it gained four stories in the 1950s. You can tell where the newer part starts—the terra-cotta becomes a lot simpler.

Turn left (southeast) on 3rd Ave. Near Pike St. is the Century Square retail and office complex (known to some as the Braun shaver building for its curved roof). Across Pike stand the onetime outposts of five-and-dime rivals Woolworth and Kress. The former now houses Ross Dress for Less; the latter's tenants include an IGA supermarket (in the basement). At Union St., a cinema that went porno in the 1970s is now the Triple Door, a posh music and cabaret joint. Beyond Union is the swank ❹ **Benaroya Hall,** home of the Seattle Symphony. It looks a lot like a streamlined modern Protestant church—if Protestant churches had huge Dale Chihuly chandeliers in their lobbies.

Turn left (northeast) on University St. On the southeast corner of 3rd Ave. and University St., the 1929 Seattle (née Northern Life) Tower is a 27-story Art Deco mountain peak. (We look more closely at it in Walk 2.) At this intersection's northwest corner, the 1910 Cobb Building is 11 stories of Beaux Arts brick cladding with a graceful curved corner. Its former block-long clone across 4th, the White-Henry-Stuart Building, was razed in the 1970s for Rainier Square, a glass-and-steel tower above an odd, tapered pedestal above ground-floor retail. Seattle architect Minoru Yamasaki, who designed New York's World Trade Center towers, also designed Rainier Square. (A second tower is being built on the block's north half.)

Paramount Theater's re-created signage

Cross 4th Ave. and walk southeast (right). To your left, the 1924 **⑤ Olympic Hotel** remains, as an old ad slogan put it, "the hotel Seattle calls home." It was once the flagship of the chain now known as Westin; the Toronto-based Fairmont Hotels currently runs it. On the following block, three newer hotels offer less-formal luxury lodgings. Beyond Spring St. two buildings, the Seattle Central Library and Safeco Plaza, bookend four decades of monumental architecture (more about them in Walk 2).

To your left, south of Madison St., stands the 901 Fifth Avenue Building, built in 1974 for the Bank of California; Bartell Drugs, on the ground floor, used to be that bank's lobby. At the end of that block, the YMCA's collegiate Gothic-style building was a 1931 addition to the 1907 original, since razed for an office tower.

To your right beyond Marion St., the Pacific (née Leamington) Hotel, a pair of 1918 low-rises, has been respectfully altered into affordable apartments. To your left from there, the ivy-covered Rainier Club has been the city's poshest private meeting and dining hall since 1904. One block farther, across Columbia St., the three concave towers of Columbia Center rise 76 stories, the tallest building west of the Mississippi.

Continue on 4th beyond Cherry St. to the 2003-vintage City Hall, a grand postmodern space with a two-level public square. A Nordic-modern city council chamber anchors its interior. If you're walking during regular business hours, you can take the elevator up to its 5th Ave. level and out its eastern exit. Otherwise, take a steep walk up James St., past the King County Administration Building (which looks a lot like an old console TV set with the doors closed).

Turn left (northwest) on 5th Ave. The police department and municipal court are in the Seattle Justice Center at 5th and James. The city bought an entire high-rise from a bankrupt developer; it's now the Seattle Municipal Tower beyond Cherry St. At the southwest corner of 5th and Marion, ❻ **The Sanctuary at the Mark** (an event space available for rent) occupies a grand 1908 Beaux Arts building, formerly First United Methodist Church.

Beyond Madison St., the 1940 Nakamura Federal Courthouse sits behind a half-block lawn that used to be downtown's biggest open space. Just before Seneca St., the 1913 YWCA building offers relief sculptures of classical Greek women reading scrolls and holding swords. Just across Seneca, the IBM Building is another Minoru Yamasaki design in understated white stripes and clean lines and curves.

North of University St., the Skinner Building somehow combines two 1920s styles: Chinese exotica and Mediterranean palazzo. The former is most prevalent inside the building's anchor space, the ❼ **5th Avenue Theatre**, another movie palace that now hosts stage musicals. (The big exterior sign is a new addition, designed to look as if it had always been there.)

To your right at 5th and Pike St., the US Bank Centre is a 1980s attempt to bring ornamental frills back to office tower architecture. Across Pike, Banana Republic occupies what had been Priteca's 1916 Coliseum Theater, which some bill as the first US building made expressly as a movie house. On the intersection's northwest side, three former Nordstrom buildings now host Urban Outfitters, Anthropologie, Allsaints, and Sephora.

Turn right (northeast) on Pike past a Sheraton hotel and recent chain-retail structures. Continue at 8th Ave. to a domed skybridge over Pike at the ❽ **Washington State Convention Center**. The skybridge wasn't there when the World Trade Organization met here in 1999. If it had been, the thousands of protesters filling the streets wouldn't have succeeded in blocking access to the place.

To return to this walk's start, walk to 9th and Pine, then take a left and continue one block.

This walk connects easily to a half dozen other walks. It crosses Walk 2 at several points. It ends three blocks southwest of Walk 6. At 5th and Pine you're three blocks southeast of Walk 7. At 3rd and Pine you're two blocks from Walk 3. At 4th and Cherry you're one block northeast of Walk 1. At 5th and Seneca you're three blocks southwest of Walk 12.

Backstory: Renamed Buildings

Many local buildings have gone through name changes because of acquisitions, rebranding, and other motivations. Many old-timers insist on using the buildings' previous names. Here's a guide to the more prominent renamings:

NOW	THEN
Nordstrom	Frederick & Nelson
Macy's	The Bon Marché
Safeco Plaza	1000 4th Avenue Plaza; Seafirst Tower
UW Tower (U District)	Safeco Plaza
Russell Investments Center	WaMu Center
Fairmont Olympic Hotel	Four Seasons Olympic; The Olympic
UW Plaza (Fourth Ave.)	Puget Sound Plaza
US Bank Centre	City Centre; Pacific First Centre
1201 Third Avenue	Washington Mutual Tower
Wells Fargo Center	First Interstate Center
Seattle Municipal Tower	AT&T Gateway Tower; Key Bank Tower
Columbia Center	Bank of America Tower; Columbia Seafirst Center
CenturyLink Plaza	1600 Bell Plaza; US West Building; Pacific Northwest Bell Building; Qwest Plaza

Points of Interest

1 **Paramount Theater** 911 Pine St., 206-682-1414, stgpresents.org

2 **Pacific Place** 600 Pine St., pacificplaceseattle.com

3 **Westlake Center** 400 Pine St., westlakecenter.com

4 **Benaroya Hall** 200 University St., 206-215-4800, seattlesymphony.org

5 **Fairmont Olympic Hotel** 411 University St., 206-621-1700, fairmont.com/seattle

6 **The Sanctuary at the Mark** 811 5th Ave., 206-800-8119, thesanctuaryseattle.com

7 **5th Avenue Theatre** 1308 5th Ave., 206-625-1900, 5thavenue.org

8 **Washington State Convention Center** 7th Ave. and Pike St., 206-694-5000, wscc.com

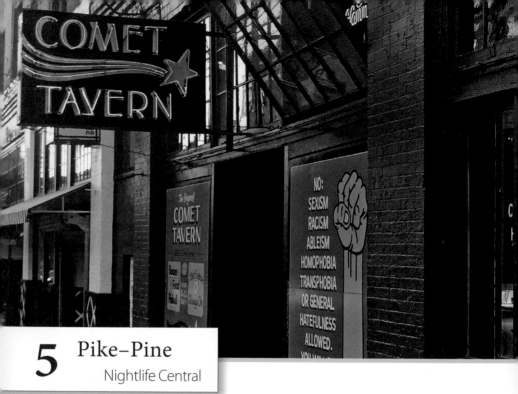

5 Pike–Pine
Nightlife Central

Above: *Comet Tavern*

BOUNDARIES: Boren Ave., E. Pike St., 16th Ave. E., and E. Pine St.
DISTANCE: 2 miles
DIFFICULTY: Moderate (half gently uphill, half gently downhill)
PARKING: Metered street parking; a pay lot on Pike east of Boren
PUBLIC TRANSIT: Metro routes 10, 11, 43, 47, and 49 stop at this walk's start; First Hill Streetcar at Broadway and Pine; light-rail Capitol Hill Station

The Pike–Pine Corridor has supplanted Broadway's dominance of the Capitol Hill business scene. Once Seattle's Auto Row, its handsome prewar showrooms and garages now house the bulk of The Hill's LGBTQ, music, art, and theater scenes, plus still more places at which to eat, drink, and shop. (As with many of this book's walks, there are far too many cool spaces to mention; take the time to make your own discoveries.) Along the way, this walk passes a major indie bookstore in a former auto-parts warehouse, a ballroom dance studio in a former Odd Fellows Hall, a literary arts center in a former funeral parlor, and two separate quartets of Greek-style architectural columns, disembodied from the houses of worship they once fronted.

Walk Description

Start at **❶ Plymouth Pillars Park,** at the northwest corner of Pike St. and Boren Ave. It overlooks I-5, the downtown skyline, Queen Anne Hill, and the Space Needle. The titular columns are from the original Plymouth Congregational Church (Walk 2), razed to make way for I-5.

Walk northeast on Pike, which bends east one block later. The architectural aesthetic is more prewar-industrial, less ostentatious, than the previous two Capitol Hill walks. You're on Seattle's original Auto Row. Ex-showroom and garage buildings now host hangout restaurants (Six Arms), gay bars (Seattle Eagle), and tourist spots (Starbucks's Reserve Roastery). East of Bellevue Ave. E., **❷ First Covenant Church** features a circular sanctuary under a gilt-tipped dome. Swedish immigrants founded the century-old congregation.

The former facade of another car dealership now fronts luxury apartments at Pike and Boylston St. Kitty-corner from there stands a three-story bay-windowed apartment complex; its street-level shops include the nationally famous sex-toy store Babeland. Beyond Pike and Harvard, the recently built Harvard Market retail complex on your right tries to fit in with the old two-story brick structures on your left.

Continue on Pike east of Broadway, through the beating heart of Seattle's art-hipster realm. Amid the poster-encrusted light poles and strewn copies of *The Stranger* newspaper, you may find the coffee crowd (Caffe Vita), the beer crowd (Comet Tavern, Elysian Brewpub), the cocktail crowd (Quinn's, Bimbo's Cantina), the cheap-eats crowd (Lost Lake, Big Mario's Pizza), the live-rock crowd (Neumo's, Chop Suey), the live-theater crowd (Annex, 12th Ave. Arts, Velocity Dance), the gay male crowd (The Unicorn), and the gay female crowd (the Wild Rose, Washington's only official lesbian bar).

The side streets here have their own attractions. North of Pike on 10th Ave. is the **❸ Elliott Bay Book Co.,** a wooden-shelved cathedral of literary mellowness. North of Pike at 11th are more hip bars, plus the acclaimed Vermillion Gallery. North of Pike on 12th is the **❹ Northwest Film Forum,** a year-round film festival and film school in one.

Turn right (south) on 15th Ave. from a long, low roadhouse structure (once C. C. Attle's gay bar). To your left is the full-block campus of **❺ Temple De Hirsch Sinai,** Seattle's principal Jewish congregation. At the end of the block, north of Union St., is a small park atop a short set of steps, with another quartet of building columns. They're from the temple's original building, razed in 1993. Take a left to walk through the park and the parking lot behind it, to 16th Ave. You can now see the temple's 1960-built Alhadeff Sanctuary with its fezlike, 14-sided dome.

Turn left (north) on 16th to the five-way intersection with E. Madison St. and E. Pine St. The big Beaux Arts building to your right is the Olympian Apartments seen in the films *House of Games* and *The Fabulous Baker Boys*. On Madison's west side is Madison Market, a natural foods co-op.

Turn left (west) on Pine. You pass some 2000s-built mixed-use behemoths. Then at the southeast corner of 14th and Pine is the ❻ **First AME Church,** Seattle's biggest historically black congregation. At 13th Ave., Cuff Complex's tiny sign is a throwback to when gay bars had to look inconspicuous. At 11th Ave., Cal Anderson Park is one of the city's most-used active-recreation parks; it was recently enlarged by covering an adjacent reservoir. In mid-2018 ❼ **Richard Hugo House,** a literary arts and education center, moved to a new building on its old site, on the east side of 11th.

Just south of Pine on 10th, the venerable Odd Fellows Hall used to have a lot of theater and dance troupes in its once-cheap spaces. It still has the Century Ballroom inside (lindy hop lessons weekly) and a swank yet homey bistro and bar outside.

At Pine and Broadway, an art supply store occupies a lavish former Pontiac dealership. In front of the store is a kitschy life-size statue of Jimi Hendrix, installed when an office-music company occupied the building. Across Broadway is ❽ **Seattle Central College**. It has won awards for its programs but not for its architecture, a slab of 1970s brutalism that replaced the grand Edwardian Broadway High School. Broadway High's auditorium annex survives as the ❾ **Broadway Performance Hall,** host to dance and theater events.

Across Pine, SCC has expanded into a former Masonic Temple. That building's main auditorium is leased to the ❿ **SIFF Cinema Egyptian;** every May it's ground zero for the Seattle International Film Festival (the biggest event of its kind in the United States).

On Pine west of Harvard Ave., Bill's Off Broadway pizza parlor starts another stretch of booze joints (Linda's, R Place, Pine Box, Sugar Hill), snack joints (Hot Mama's Pizza), and caffeine joints (another Victrola Coffee). There's unique shopping here too—Asian and Indian gifts, retro-modern furniture, young fashions, and rare LPs.

Pine bends southwest at Melrose Ave., by the posh dance club The Baltic Room. Just beyond Minor Ave., take a left turn back into Plymouth Pillars Park. This section has an off-leash dog park space and some oversize concrete urns from the old Music Hall theater downtown (demolished in 1992). You're just across Boren from your start.

This walk connects easily to a half dozen other walks. It starts and ends across the I-5 overpass from Walks 2 and 4. At Broadway and Pike you're one block north of Walk 6. At 16th and Union you're two blocks west of Walk 12. At 13th and Pine you're one block south of Walk 11. At Bellevue and Pine you're two blocks south of Walk 10.

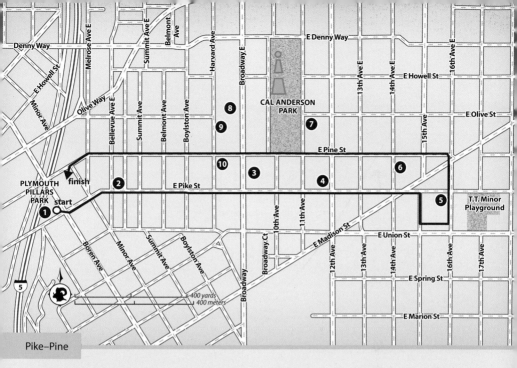

Points of Interest

1 **Plymouth Pillars Park** 1050 Pike St., seattle.gov/parks/find/parks/plymouth-pillars-park

2 **First Covenant Church** 400 E. Pike St., 206-322-7411, firstcovenantseattle.org

3 **Elliott Bay Book Co.** 1521 10th Ave., 206-624-6600, elliottbaybook.com

4 **Northwest Film Forum** 1515 12th Ave., 206-329-2629, nwfilmforum.org

5 **Temple De Hirsch Sinai** 1511 E. Pike St., 206-323-8486, tdhs-nw.org

6 **First AME Church** 1522 14th Ave., 206-324-3664, fameseattle.org

7 **Richard Hugo House** 1634 11th Ave., 206-322-7030, hugohouse.org

8 **Seattle Central College** 1701 Broadway, 206-934-3800, seattlecentral.edu

9 **Broadway Performance Hall** 1625 Broadway, 206-934-3052, theatres.seattlecentral.edu/broadway-performance-hall

10 **SIFF Cinema Egyptian** 805 E. Pine St., 206-464-5830, siff.net/cinema

6 First Hill
Priests and Pills

Above: *Stimson-Green Mansion*

BOUNDARIES: 12th Ave., Seneca St., 8th Ave., and E. Union St.
DISTANCE: 2.25 miles
DIFFICULTY: Moderate (mostly flat or downhill)
PARKING: Metered street parking; a pay lot
PUBLIC TRANSIT: Metro routes 2, 12, 20, and 60 stop near this walk's start; First Hill Streetcar at
   Broadway and Marion

"Seattle's 1st Neighborhood," as promotional street banners call it, is a residential neighborhood overlooking downtown. Once the timber came down from these slopes in the late 19th century, prestigious big homes went up; four of them are still standing as restored historic sites. It's also informally known as Pill Hill, with most of Seattle's major hospitals, and as Catholic Hill, with several major ecclesiastical institutions, including the city's principal cathedral, a Jesuit university campus, and an angular modern chapel. You also pass art spaces devoted to realist painting and contemporary photography, and a stunning century-old hotel.

Walk Description

Start at the northwest corner of Terry Ave. and Madison St., just outside the ❶ **Hotel Sorrento**'s grand courtyard. The Italian villa–style boutique hotel is another legacy from the 1909 Alaska-Yukon-Pacific Exposition (Walk 25). If you have the time, peek inside at the sumptuous lobby and Fireside Room.

Head northeast on Madison for one block. To your left are two old, terra-cotta clad, single-story retail buildings. To your right is a recent mixed-use behemoth. At Boren Ave., the University Club of Seattle occupies a grand old turn-of-the-last-century mansion, behind some thick shrubbery.

Turn left (northwest) onto Boren Ave. and continue for two blocks. To your left, the Hideout is a dark, tastefully signed storefront bar that's become a hangout for the local art scene. To your right at Boren and Spring, the William Hofius House (a 1902 foursquare-style mansion) is now Connolly House, headquarters to the Catholic archbishop of Seattle.

Turn right (northeast) on Seneca St. and continue for four blocks. Among this stretch's elegant old apartment buildings are two more vintage mansions. The 1907 Dearborn House, at the southwest corner of Seneca and Minor Ave., is now home to the preservation group Historic Seattle. Kitty-corner from there, the 1899 ❷ **Stimson-Green Mansion** is owned by another nonprofit, the Washington Trust for Historic Preservation, and is a popular wedding and party site.

At the five-way intersection of Seneca, Harvard Ave., and Union St., see the noble ❸ **Seattle First Baptist Church** (built in stages from 1910 to 1920), with its gentle juxtaposition of curves and angles. Dogleg left along Harvard toward Union, at a dark brick Knights of Columbus hall.

Turn right (east) on Union, the cusp between the First Hill and Capitol Hill neighborhoods. The Cancer Pathways support center (formerly Gilda's Club, named for comedienne Gilda Radner) sits at Broadway and Union. The former law-office building's front replicates the front of Thomas Jefferson's home in Monticello, Virginia. Looking south from there, Garage is a bar and pool hall that also has some of Seattle's last public bowling lanes.

On the southeast side of 10th Ave. and Union, a weathered old commercial building juxta-poses an auto-repair shop with an art gallery, a tattoo parlor, and a fringe-theater studio. Directly east of that building is the pizza joint Sizzle Pie. Looking south of Union on 10th, you can glimpse Seattle's last blue-roofed IHOP restaurant.

At the six-way intersection of Union, 12th Ave., and Madison St. are two extremes in contemporary nightlife—Tavern Law, a very inconspicuous neo-speakeasy, and Pony, a very visible gay dance club. Turn right (south) on 12th, past the Seattle Academy of Arts and Sciences (a private secondary school), Café Presse (a soccer bar and espresso joint), and ❹ **Photographic Center Northwest** (where members and students still take pictures with film).

Turn right (west) on E. Marion St. and walk through the campus of ❺ **Seattle University.** One block into the grounds, look right to see a reflecting pool in front of the Chapel of St. Ignatius. Architect Steven Holl designed the Jesuit university's first on-campus church in the 1990s; it's a meditative masterwork of light, color, and juxtaposed shapes. Many critics compare it favorably to another local work of postmodern asymmetry, the Museum of Pop Culture (Walk 7).

Continue westward through SU, past a pleasant mix of 1920s, 1960s, and 1990s structures. At this point your path turns moderately uphill, including three short sets of stairs. Just before you leave the campus grounds at Broadway, you see a bust of Chief Seattle to your right.

St. James Cathedral

Turn left (south) on Broadway. You soon see the grand entrance to Swedish Medical Center, the crown of Pill Hill. Cross Broadway at Columbia St. for a closer look at the gently curving white front of this massive health care complex.

Turn southwest on Cherry St., through the Swedish campus. Across Boren, you see banners promoting the **6** **Frye Art Museum**. Continue to the Frye's main entrance at Terry Ave. and Cherry. Funded by the estate of meatpacking moguls Charles and Emma Frye, and originally dedicated to realist painting, it now hosts a variety of contemporary and classical exhibits. Even if you don't stop in (admission's always free), the front plaza's a pleasant spot to relax before resuming your journey.

Turn right (northwest) on Terry. You're soon flanked by the buildings of O'Dea High, a parochial boys' school founded in 1923. On your left as you approach Marion St., **7** **St. James Cathedral** looks spectacular even from the back.

Turn left on Marion and left again on 9th Ave. for a full view of St. James's exterior. The Italian Renaissance–style edifice originally opened in 1907; it's been revamped, inside and out, several times. Still here from the beginning are the grand staircase and the two square, 167-foot towers in front. The bronze doors were added in 1999. The interior is even more magnificent; tours are held weekly during summer.

Continue southeast on 9th. On your right south of Cherry, the German Heritage Society is ensconced in an 1885 U.S. Assay Office, a two-story painted brick building with quaint Old West flourishes.

Two blocks from there, Harborview Medical Center's 1931 institutional Art Deco has been compromised a bit with recent additions, including a six-story, glass-walled skybridge across 9th. South of the skybridge, the Moderne design motif remains, both in the main hospital to your right and in the Harborview Hall annex to your left (originally a nurses' dormitory).

Backtrack on 9th to James St. and turn left, for one seriously downhill block. At 8th Ave. and James, the 1890 **8** **Trinity Episcopal Church** is an English Gothic masterwork clad in rough stone.

Turn right (northwest) on 8th Ave. At Spring St., First Presbyterian is one of Seattle's oldest congregations (founded in 1869), with a stunning mid-century modern edifice.

Approaching Seneca St., **9** **Town Hall Seattle** hosts lectures, panels, and recitals in a stucco-clad former Christian Science church (one of five reused Christian Science buildings described in this book). From here you're two uphill blocks away from Terry.

This walk connects easily with four other walks. At 12th and Union you're one block south of Walk 5 and six blocks west of Walk 12. This walk ends one block northeast of Walk 2 and three blocks northeast of Walk 4.

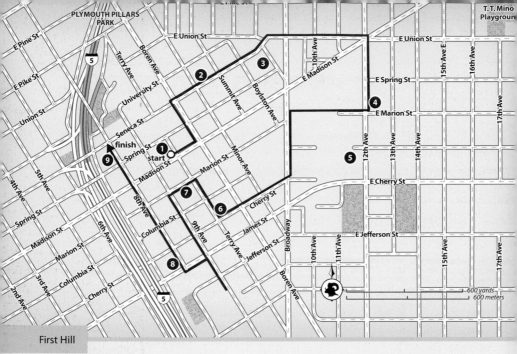

Points of Interest

① Hotel Sorrento 900 Madison St., 206-622-6400, hotelsorrento.com

② Stimson-Green Mansion 1204 Minor Ave., 206-624-0474, stimsongreen.com

③ Seattle First Baptist Church 1111 Harvard Ave., 206-325-6051, seattlefirstbaptist.org

④ Photographic Center Northwest 900 12th Ave., 206-720-7222, pcnw.org

⑤ Seattle University 901 12th Ave., 206-296-6000, seattleu.edu

⑥ Frye Art Museum 704 Terry Ave., 206-622-9250, fryemuseum.org

⑦ St. James Cathedral 804 9th Ave., 206-622-3559, stjames-cathedral.org

⑧ Trinity Episcopal Church 609 8th Ave., 206-624-5337, trinityseattle.org

⑨ Town Hall Seattle 1119 8th Ave., 206-652-4255, townhallseattle.org

7 Belltown and Seattle Center
Under the Needle

BOUNDARIES: 5th Ave., Virginia St., Warren Ave. N., and Mercer St.
DISTANCE: 4 miles, in 2 segments
DIFFICULTY: Easy (all flat or slight inclines)
PARKING: Metered street parking; pay lots along Denny Way east of Broad St.
PUBLIC TRANSIT: Metro routes 3, 4, and 8 stop near 5th and Denny; many others stop
    2 blocks west on 3rd.

In 1962 local civic leaders mounted the Century 21 Exposition, a world's fair celebrating what our society was supposed to have become by now. While we don't yet have domed cities or flying cars, we have kept the fair's grounds as a place for theater, opera, sports, science exhibits, and festivals. It all occurs under the watchful gaze and wasp-waisted stance of the Space Needle, one of the world's most recognizable icons. Seattle's prime symbol also presides over Belltown and the Denny Regrade, neighborhoods that many have long overlooked. Where the fair's monorail once passed above car lots, printing plants, and nondescript commercial buildings, residential towers now scrape the sky and fashionable restaurants and boutiques beckon.

Walk Description

Start at Tilikum Place Park at the triangle of 5th Ave., Cedar St., and Denny Way. You're near what was the northern end of Denny Hill. The steep hill rose more than 100 feet, impeding the city's northern growth in the horse-and-wagon days. It was removed in three massive regrades from 1906 to 1929.

Since 1912, cobblestoned Tilikum Place has been home to a statue of the city's namesake, Chief Seattle (also spelled Sealth and Si'ahl in the imprecise transliteration of his Lushootseed language). His arm is outstretched to welcome the first white settlers—not necessarily to lead them to the ❶ **5 Point Café** (a lovingly preserved 24-hour dive diner and bar).

Turn right (southeast) along 5th Ave. You're underneath the bulky concrete track of the monorail, created to bring world's fair visitors to the downtown core. At Wall St., the 1948 *Post-Intelligencer* building, a full-block slab of Truman-era concrete, is now gussied up for the for-profit City University. On 5th's southwest side between Bell and Blanchard is the ❷ **Seattle Glassblowing Studio,** where you can buy decorative glass art and watch it being made.

Beyond 5th Ave. and Blanchard St., Top Pot Doughnuts occupies a stunning glass-fronted mid-century building. At Lenora St., look to your left to see three connected giant glass spheres anchoring one of Amazon's new office towers.

Seattle Glassblowing Studio offers classes and sells hand-blown and hand-sculpted glass art.

At Virginia St. looms the twin-cylindered ❸ **Westin Hotel**. The formerly Seattle-based chain has been at this location since 1928. The current towers were built in 1969 and 1982.

Turn right (southwest) along Virginia. At 4th Ave. lies Escala, one of the most grandiose of our late-2000s condo megaprojects. (It's the fictional setting for the *Fifty Shades of Grey* novels, though the film versions were shot in Vancouver.)

Virginia and 4th also is ground zero for celebrity restaurateur Tom Douglas, with his creations Lola, Dahlia Lounge, Dahlia Bakery, and Serious Pie. A neon sign depicting Douglas holding a wriggling fish hangs outside Dahlia Lounge. Sub Pop, the record label that turned grunge music into a worldwide craze, has its offices in that building.

Turn right (northwest) along 4th. The 1963 Cinerama theater at Lenora St. is a plain box on the outside but a streamlined movie palace inside. On the same block is Yuki's Diffusion hair salon, run by Yuki Ohno, father of speed-skating champ Apolo Anton Ohno.

Turn left (southwest) at 4th Ave. and Battery St. The handsome, brick-clad Fire Station 2 is the oldest station in the city still operating. Kitty-corner from there, the black-glassed Fourth and Battery Building is Belltown's earliest "new" office tower (built in 1974). Two blocks away, at 2nd Ave., Buckley's sports bar inhabits an Art Deco gem that was once MGM's regional office. This stretch of 2nd is Film Row, a onetime hotbed of distribution offices, film vaults, and theater-supply companies.

Turn left (southeast) along 2nd. City Hostel Seattle, next to Buckley's, was originally the William Tell Hotel, where studio sales reps (and at least a few movie stars) stayed while visiting Film Row. Across 2nd, the Rendezvous restaurant and lounge was originally a theater design and building company; its exquisite Jewel Box Theatre was that company's showroom.

At 2nd and Bell St., Mama's Cantina is an upscale iteration of its funkier predecessor but still has some of the old Mama's Elvis-dominated kitsch decor. It starts a block of hip drinking and music spots. ❹ **The Crocodile,** one of Seattle's top rock clubs for two decades, stands at the block's other end at 2nd and Blanchard. One block away at 2nd and Lenora, the facade of the 1914 Crystal Pool now anchors a condo tower.

A block away at Virginia St., the ❺ **Moore Theatre,** a magnificent 1907 vaudeville palace, still hosts touring concerts and shows. Its ground-floor storefronts include the Fancy boutique (jewelry and metal decorative pieces). Turn right (southwest) along Virginia to 1st Ave. and the Terminal Sales Building (Walk 3).

Turn right (northwest) along 1st and proceed 11 blocks to enjoy Seattle's prime see-and-be-seen nightlife. These joints range from loud DJ clubs to swank wine bars to quiet supper clubs to fashionably dark cocktail houses to boisterous meet-markets to smarty-arty hangouts to former dive bars gone legit. Many of these are open for daytime dining. This stretch of 1st Ave. also offers fashionable shopping, including clothes, pet supplies, and home furnishings.

And there's plenty of classic architecture among the newer condos—the Vogue Hotel (now the Vain hair salon), the 1889 Odd Fellows Hall (now a pub), the 1889 Hull Building (now a fashion boutique), the Austin A. Bell Building (whose facade now stands in front of a condo structure), the Sailors Union of the Pacific (now a bar, restaurant, and movie theater), the Electrical Workers' hall (now a church), and the King County Labor Temple (still union offices!).

Turn right (east) along Denny Way's north side, and continue five blocks, to Broad St. You pass the new First United Methodist Church (a modern replacement for the building that is now The Sanctuary at the Mark, Walk 4).

If you'd like to stop, take Denny back to 5th Ave. If you're continuing, turn left (northeast) at Denny and Broad for less than a block, to ❻ **Seattle Center**'s first pedestrian entrance.

Take a left and meander north through this pathway, toward the ❼ **Space Needle**. Along the way you pass through *Olympic Iliad,* Alexander Liberman's sculpture made from orange metal tubes. You also pass a meditation garden donated by the Sri Chinmoy Foundation.

Turn right (east) at the Space Needle's north side, parallel to its main entrance. Even if you don't visit the 605-foot tower's restaurant or observation deck, you can admire the graceful curves of its tripod and UFO-esque top. To the Space Needle's west is ❽ **Chihuly Garden and Glass,** a permanent exhibit of glass sculptures by Seattle's most famous visual artist.

Turn left (north) in front of the west side of the ❾ **Museum of Pop Culture (MoPOP),** with exhibits about music, science fiction, comics, and so on. Microsoft cofounder Paul Allen commissioned architect Frank Gehry's bold structure (designed without straight corners) as a tribute to rock music (and, some claim, to Allen's ego).

From MoPOP's western entrance walk left (west), into the east entrance of the 1939-built Armory building, one of several prefair buildings that were incorporated into the Century 21 grounds. Take the stairs up to its main floor and food court, known during the fair as the Food Circus. Exit at the Armory's west side.

Turn right to head north past the International Fountain, a 1985 replacement for the fair's high-streaming centerpiece spectacle. Turn right (east) at the Kobe Bell (a gift from Seattle's Japanese sister city) into the elaborately lit courtyard of McCaw Hall. Home to Seattle Opera and Pacific Northwest Ballet, it's the third incarnation of the 1928 Civic Auditorium.

Backtrack to the courtyard's south end and turn right (west), toward the Bagley Wright Theatre (home of the Seattle Repertory Theatre with its curvy, glassy front side). Continue west to the Center's Warren Ave. N./Republican St. entrance. An open wooden doorway planted here is a memorial to renowned playwright August Wilson.

Turn left (south) and head down a small flight of outdoor stairs, through a passage between the two Northwest Court buildings. These exhibit spaces are now home to the Vera Project (a teen-centric arts center), SIFF Film Center (a year-round extension of the Seattle International

Backstory: The Regrade

Belltown's walkability results from Seattle's own *Extreme Makeover: City Edition*. Early city leaders decided that 100-foot-tall Denny Hill, just northwest of downtown, stood in the way of urban growth because horse-drawn wagons could not carry merchandise over it. From 1902 to 1911, some 27 blocks were sluiced down flat. By the time it was done, the Ford Model T had made horse-drawn delivery obsolete. The rest of the hill, from Fifth to Westlake Aves., was steam-shoveled away from 1929 to 1930.

Film Festival), and ❿ **KEXP** (a world-renowned eclectic radio station, with a La Marzocco café in its public Gathering Space room). Take a right (east) and then another right (south) beside KeyArena, created in 1995 with components from the fair-era coliseum. It was built because the SuperSonics basketball team said they'd leave town without a new arena. Thirteen years later they left anyway. (It's now being rebuilt again.) Continue south to Thomas St.

Turn left to head east along the back of Fisher Pavilion, which is built into a hillside. Its entire roof is an outdoor plaza.

Turn right (south) in front of Seattle Children's Theatre (also known as the Charlotte Martin Theatre), a handsome 1993 addition to a 1956 Shrine temple. You soon reach the main entrance to ⓫ **Pacific Science Center**. Minoru Yamasaki (Walk 4) designed this sextet of clean white boxes with his trademark vertical trim features, surrounding reflecting pools, and streamlined, Gothic-inspired arches. Its recently added IMAX Dome screens first-run 3D movies.

Turn left (east), past the south side of the Mural Amphitheater, a performance space with Paul Horiuchi's 60-foot-long *Seattle Mural* as its backdrop.

Continue east to the Space Needle's south side. Turn right (southeast) through a circular plaza surrounding a fountain. Leave the Center at the triangular intersection of Broad St., John St., and 4th Ave. N.

Cross Broad St. toward KOMO Plaza. Walk a southeasterly dogleg between its two buildings. At the northwest corner of 5th and Denny you can see the Needle framed by satellite dishes on KOMO Plaza's roof. Before you cross Denny back to Tilikum Place, look east for the pink neon sign announcing the Elephant Super Car Wash.

This walk connects easily to three other walks. At 4th and Virginia you're two blocks northwest of Walk 4. At 1st and Virginia you're at the start of Walk 3. At Warren and Republican you're one block east of Walk 18.

Points of Interest

1. **5 Point Café** 415 Cedar St., 206-448-9991, the5pointcafe.com

2. **Seattle Glassblowing Studio** 2227 5th Ave., 206-448-2181, seattleglassblowing.com

3. **Westin Seattle** 1900 5th Ave., 206-728-1000, starwoodhotels.com/westin/seattle

4. **The Crocodile** 2200 2nd Ave., 206-441-4618, thecrocodile.com

5. **Moore Theatre** 1932 2nd Ave., 206-682-1414, stgpresents.org

6. **Seattle Center** 305 Harrison St., 206-684-7200, seattlecenter.com

7. **Space Needle** 400 Broad St., 206-905-2100, spaceneedle.com

8. **Chihuly Garden and Glass** 305 Harrison St., 206-753-4940, chihulygardenandglass.com

9. **Museum of Pop Culture (MoPOP)** 325 5th Ave. N., 206-770-2700, mopop.org

10. **KEXP and La Marzocco** 472 1st Ave. N., 206-520-5800, kexp.org

11. **Pacific Science Center** 200 2nd Ave. N., 206-443-2001, pacsci.org

8 South Lake Union
Shiny and Techy

Above: Cornish College of the Arts' Raisbeck Performance Hall

BOUNDARIES: Boren Ave. N., Eastlake Ave. N., Fairview Ave. N., Valley St., and Westlake Ave. N.
DISTANCE: 2.75 miles
DIFFICULTY: Moderate (2 brief uphill segments, 1 toward the end)
PARKING: Metered street parking; pay lots and garages include a lot at Boren Ave. and Lenora St.
PUBLIC TRANSIT: The Seattle Streetcar stops at 9th Ave., Westlake Ave., and Blanchard St. Metro routes 8 and 70 stop along Fairview Ave. N.

This former low-rent district northeast of downtown has blossomed, thanks in part to Microsoft cofounder Paul Allen's real estate ventures. Many big and shiny office, residential, and retail projects have turned much of South Lake Union into a high-tech fantasy land, complete with its own neighborhood trolley. That's not to say there was nothing there before. For decades, city officials vowed to maintain Lake Union as a "working lake," and the blocks south of the lake still hold on to some of their industrial history and a particular rustic beauty. It's a place where one of the original grunge music clubs, an ornate little orthodox church, and a mammoth nonprofit outdoors store coexist in mutual tolerance.

Walk Description

Start at Boren Ave. N. and John St. outside the shrinking offices of the *Seattle Times* in an old furniture warehouse. The 1930 Moderne facade of the *Times*'s former headquarters, across Boren on John, is preserved while a new tower goes up behind it.

Walk south to Boren and Denny Way. Dogleg left, then right, on Denny and back onto Boren, walking southeast. You soon find the gently sloped wood structure that's now Cornish College of the Arts' ❶ **Raisbeck Performance Hall**. The 1915 timbered structure was originally a Sons of Norway Hall; later it housed a series of gay dance clubs.

Turn left (northeast) at Boren and Howell St. On Howell's south side, the older of Martin Selig's two Metropolitan Park office buildings is known as the Can of Spam Building. Across from it is ❷ **Re-bar,** for more than two decades a straight and gay crossover DJ club and performance space. (It's where columnist Dan Savage once directed drag productions of female-lead stage plays.) The building also houses the Market House Deli, selling the best corned beef in town.

Continue as Howell bends left (north) into Eastlake Ave. Just beyond the Denny Way overpass is a long, gritty structure that's been a live music venue for more than four decades. It's now ❸ **El Corazón,** but it was the Off Ramp when all the pre-stardom grunge bands played there.

Across Eastlake and John St. is the massive retail theater spectacle that is the flagship ❹ **REI (Recreational Equipment Inc.)** store. The sporting goods giant began as a cooperative buying service, outfitting serious mountain climbers. It has a big climbing wall and an outdoor trail network (for test-riding mountain bikes and hiking shoes).

Cross the south side of the REI complex, to Yale Ave. north of John. Cross Yale to Alley24, a full-block residential, retail, and office complex incorporating the brick facade of an old laundry building. It includes Lunchbox Laboratory, a gourmet burger emporium that moved here from Ballard to be near the office crowd.

Exit Alley24 at its north side. Turn left (west) on Thomas St. Beyond the intersection with Pontius Ave. N. (nobody's opened a Pilates studio on that street yet), the Cascade Playground and P-Patch combines green space with a community garden and a meeting hall. On the south side of Thomas, enjoy the century-old ❺ **Immanuel Lutheran Church,** a solid bulk of white-painted wood construction.

The Seattle Streetcar, also known as South Lake Union Trolley

Turn right (north) on Minor, and go one block to Harrison St., in view of the P-Patch and its adjacent Garden of Happiness. Turn right (east) on Harrison and go two blocks to Yale Ave. The exquisite brick ❻ **St. Spiridon Orthodox Cathedral,** built in 1937, was designed in the Russian church style. It's even more stunning inside; the sanctuary is a tiny gem of art and iconography.

Turn left (north) on Yale, and continue one block to Republican St., past a new building with a German pub on its ground floor. Dogleg right (east) on Republican one block back to Eastlake. (This block's a steep climb, but just for 200 feet.) At this intersection's southwest corner are two live music bars, the Lo-Fi and Victory Lounge.

Go left and walk north on the west side of Eastlake, parallel to I-5. North of Mercer St. is a classic brick apartment block. Continue on Eastlake on an overpass above the I-5 Mercer exit (the Mercer Mess to generations of frustrated commuters), to Aloha St. You're in cancer country, the adjoining campuses of the Fred Hutchinson Cancer Research Center and the Seattle Cancer Care Alliance.

Turn left (west) on Aloha, and continue one block to Yale Ave. Turn right (north) and walk one block to the traffic circle in front of the "Hutch" campus to see *Vessel,* artist Ed Carpenter's four-story sculpture made with colorful light tubes reaching toward the sky. Turn left (west) from the traffic circle onto Ward St. heading westbound, and go one block to Fairview Ave. N. Cross Fairview to the pedestrian and bicycle path on its northwest side.

Turn left (southwest) on Fairview, near the lake. You can see yacht docks from a distance here; if you want to see them up close, turn into the **❼ Chandler's Cove Marina** complex. It includes a small private park, shops, and restaurants. Shortly beyond, the Fairview path bends south, connecting to Valley St. Look southeast at Valley and Fairview to see a stoic five-story brick building. It was originally a Ford Model T assembly plant; it later housed magazine printing presses and is now rental storage units.

Continue on the path north of Valley past Daniel's Broiler (a water-view steakhouse) and the **❽ Center for Wooden Boats** and Northwest Seaport (two nonprofits preserving Seattle's seagoing heritage). See the new Lake Union Park, a vast open space hugging the lakeshore. The park's centerpiece is a large old naval armory housing the **❾ Museum of History and Industry (MOHAI)**. Sometimes called Seattle's attic, it's a highly accessible source to the city's short but colorful heritage.

Along this path north of Terry and west of Boren is a stop for the Seattle Streetcar, a 1.3-mile high-tech trolley installed at Paul Allen's urging. Some give it the unofficial nickname South Lake Union Trolley, usually referred to by its acronym. Take the trolley west and then south on Westlake Ave. to Denny Way. Or walk this eight-block segment. If you walk it, you'll get to view many shiny new projects built for Allen and other developers.

On the east side of Westlake, south of Denny, a new complex contains a Whole Foods Market and a Pan Pacific Hotel. Climb the steps or take the elevator here, to Terry Ave. Across Terry is the hulking, tall warehouse building that's now the main campus of **❿ Cornish College of the Arts.** Founded by Nellie Cornish in 1914 as a music academy, the college now teaches visual and performing arts, interior and graphic design, and video production.

Turn right (southeast) on Terry (a slight incline) to Virginia St.; turn left and follow Virginia back to Fairview.

This walk connects easily to three other walks. Its midpoint at Fairview and Ward is near the start of Walk 9. It ends five blocks from Walk 4 and six blocks from Walk 7.

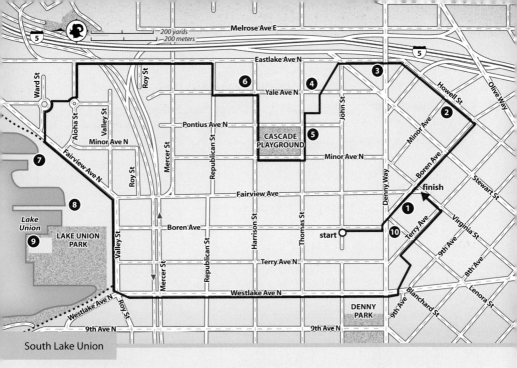

South Lake Union

Points of Interest

1 **Raisbeck Performance Hall** 2015 Boren Ave., 206-726-2787, cornish.edu/campus/raisbeck_performance_hall

2 **Re-bar** 1114 Howell St., 206-223-9873, rebarseattle.com

3 **El Corazón** 109 Eastlake Ave. E., 206-262-0482, elcorazonseattle.com

4 **REI** 222 Yale Ave. N., 206-223-1944, rei.com/stores

5 **Immanuel Lutheran Church** 1215 Thomas St., 206-622-1930, immanuelseattle.org

6 **St. Spiridon Orthodox Cathedral** 400 Yale Ave. N., 206-624-5341, saintspiridon.org

7 **Chandler's Cove Marina** 901 Fairview Ave. N., 206-420-4894

8 **Center for Wooden Boats** 1010 Valley St., 206-382-2628, cwb.org

9 **Museum of History and Industry (MOHAI)** 860 Terry Ave. N., 206-324-1126, mohai.org

10 **Cornish College of the Arts** 1000 Lenora St., 800-726-2787, cornish.edu

9 Fairview and Eastlake
On and in the Lake

Above: Wandesforde Dock and floating homes ("houseboats")

BOUNDARIES: Fairview Ave. E., Ward St., Eastlake Ave. E., and E. Roanoke St.
DISTANCE: 2.25 miles
DIFFICULTY: Easy (1 short uphill stretch)
PARKING: Pay lot at Fairview and Yale Ave. N.
PUBLIC TRANSIT: Metro route 70 and the Lake Union Streetcar stop near this walk's start.

In old Japan, the term *floating world* referred to nomadic aristocrats who were untethered to the land or to the rural economy. In Seattle, it's a close-knit subculture of a few hundred affluent households living in houseboats, as glorified in the film *Sleepless in Seattle*. About half of these houseboats are moored along the east side of Lake Union, indirectly but securely attached to the urban shore. This walk gets you as close to these dockside abodes as you are legally permitted. You will also see kayaks, seaplanes, a restored former power plant, and the city's oldest public school.

Walk Description

Start on the west side of Fairview Ave. N. at Ward St., walking northeast along Lake Union. To your left, the northern reaches of the South Lake Union restaurant strip are mixed in with yacht moorage docks. You soon find a few steps to descend, onto a floating sidewalk over an inlet. To your right is the former Lake Union Steam Plant, built by Seattle City Light between 1912 and 1928. It was later headquarters for the biotech company ZymoGenetics. As part of the remodel, lightweight replicas replaced the plant's tall smokestacks.

Once you're back on solid ground, the ❶ **Seattle Seaplanes** dock appears to your left. If you have the money, they'll take you on a 20-minute scenic flight. Fairview forks here with Eastlake Ave. E. Keep left to stay on Fairview.

The next long pier complex up ahead is home to the ❷ **Lake Union Dry Dock Co**. The shipyard and boat-repair facility is one of the last remnants of Lake Union's heritage as a "working lake."

North of that, the houseboat docks start. These aren't boats; they're houses on rafts, semipermanently moored to their docks. Seattle has about 500 floating-home moorage slots, down from more than 2,000 in the 1940s. Increased demand and limited supply have mostly turned them from artsy bohemian digs into the upscale professional abodes seen in *Sleepless in Seattle*.

On the east side of Fairview at E. Lynn St. you can get refreshments at ❸ **Pete's Wines,** formerly Pete's Supermarket. As the nomenclature implies, it's evolved over the past four decades from a grocery with a good wine selection to a major wine shop with a fair grocery selection. You can consume nonalcoholic purchases across the street at ❹ **Lynn Street Mini Park,** a lakefront park established by the store's founder, Pete Omalanz. It's festooned with tile art pieces, the product of a 2003 community campaign. Some of the tiles depict the joys of wine in memory of the late *Seattle Times* wine critic and houseboat resident Tom Stockley. Neighbors fought the Seattle Parks Department to keep those tiles installed.

A short bit north of the park, the ❺ **Floating Homes Association** (a houseboat owners' advocacy group) operates a volunteer-run gift shop, the Houseboatique. Here you can buy posters and books about houseboats and learn about the lifestyle and its 100-year history.

This stretch of Fairview ends with a right turn onto E. Roanoke St. To your left, you see more houseboat docks, plus some ritzy new lakefront townhomes. Three moderately uphill blocks later, you're at Eastlake Ave. E., the neighborhood's main arterial. Across from you is ❻ **Rogers Playground.** Behind that is Seward School, the Seattle School District's oldest extant site. It now houses an alternative elementary program, The Options Program at Seward (TOPS).

Seattle Seaplanes dock

Turn right (south) on Eastlake. This street, once little more than a byway between downtown and the U District, saw a lot of redevelopment during the 2000s. It's now dotted with recent office, apartment, and mixed-use structures. Among the surviving older businesses here are the **❼ 14 Carrot Cafe** (a hippie-esque bistro), the **❽ Eastlake Zoo Tavern** (a hippie-esque bar, more spacious and more brightly lit than most), and **❾ Patrick's Fly Shop** (fishing gear). Tiles embedded in Eastlake's sidewalks depict indigenous local plants and insects.

South of Eastlake and E. Howe St. is the Bonneville Broadcasting Building, home to longtime news-talk leader KIRO-FM. A short detour east on Howe leads to a long set of outdoor steps, heading under the I-5 overpass and up the west slope of Capitol Hill (Walk 10).

Take a right at Eastlake and E. Galer St., returning to Fairview just north of the old steam plant. Backtrack south on Fairview to your start, or take a 70 bus.

The walk connects easily to two other walks. It starts at Walk 8's midpoint. Its midpoint is 0.5 mile south of Walk 27's end.

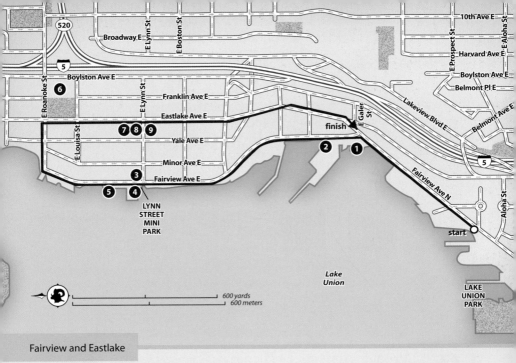

Points of Interest

1. **Seattle Seaplanes** 1325 Fairview Ave. E., 206-329-9638, seattleseaplanes.com

2. **Lake Union Drydock Co.** 1515 Fairview Ave. E., ludd.com

3. **Pete's Wines** 58 E. Lynn St., 206-322-2660, peteswineshop.com

4. **Lynn Street Mini Park** 2291 Fairview Ave. E., seattle.gov/parks/find/parks/lynn-street-mini-park

5. **Floating Homes Association** 2329 Fairview Ave. E., 206-323-3489, seattlefloatinghomes.org

6. **Rogers Playground** 2516 Eastlake Ave. E., 206-684-4075, seattle.gov/parks/find/parks/rogers-playground

7. **14 Carrot Cafe** 2305 Eastlake Ave. E., 206-324-1442

8. **Eastlake Zoo Tavern** 2301 Eastlake Ave. E., 206-329-3277, eastlakezoo.com

9. **Patrick's Fly Shop** 2237 Eastlake Ave. E., 206-325-8988, patricksflyshop.com

10 West Capitol Hill and Broadway

"Capitol" of Cool

Above: A mansion on Summit Ave. E.

BOUNDARIES: Federal Ave. E., E. Galer St., Bellevue Ave. E., and E. Olive Way
DISTANCE: 2.25 miles
DIFFICULTY: Moderate (2 modest inclines)
PARKING: Free street parking
PUBLIC TRANSIT: Metro route 47 stops at this walk's start; route 49 stops near it on Broadway;
  light-rail Capitol Hill Station at Broadway and John; First Hill Streetcar at Broadway and Denny

This walk reveals The Hill in all its diverse glory. And along the way you'll see some great architecture, including a monumental and deliberately unfinished Episcopalian church, some more sumptuous old-money mansions, and the eccentric masterworks of a highly individualistic apartment designer. You end up on Broadway, The Hill's traditional main drag. While the street's undergone a lot of changes and revamps in recent years, it remains a vital eating, shopping, and people-watching corridor.

Walk Description

Start on the northwest corner of Summit Ave. E. and E. Mercer St. in front of a couple of local hangout bars and the handsomely decked-out original location of ❶ **Top Pot Doughnuts**. Head north on Summit for two blocks, past some classic box houses and unpretentious low-rise apartments.

This stretch of Summit ends at Belmont Ave. E. In front of you is one of the idiosyncratic apartment buildings that self-taught architect Frederick Anhalt designed and built in the 1920s. His projects are known for Tudor- and Norman-inspired design flourishes and for central courtyards, bestowing a sense of community. Cross Belmont for a better view of this and another Anhalt building to its right.

Dogleg left (northwest) briefly on Belmont, right (north) on another brief piece of Summit, right (northeast) very briefly on Bellevue Pl. E., then left (north) again on yet another segment of Summit. This area is part of the Harvard-Belmont Landmark District, full of large, well-preserved old homes. One particular highlight is the relatively small Bower/Bystrom House, a blue-and-white gingerbread cottage above a street-level garage.

Continue as Summit bends northeast. This stretch is a narrow road with big curbside trees in front of even bigger prewar houses.

Summit becomes E. Prospect St., bending southeast. As you round this corner you see the back of the O. W. Fisher and O. D. Fisher houses. These exquisite Tudor manses were built for the family that once owned flour mills and KOMO-TV (Walk 7). A closer view can be had as you pass the intersection with Belmont Pl. E.

Prospect turns east (and slightly uphill) at the next intersection. To your left is a brick wall marking the original southern boundary of Horace C. Henry's estate. He was the railroad baron who funded the UW's Henry Art Gallery (Walk 25).

Turn left (north) on Harvard Ave. E. To your left, you see more of the former Henry property behind a hedge. But you won't see Henry's mansion; it was razed in 1937. Farther up the street to your right, the new Harvard and Highland condo buildings try to fit in with their surroundings with a surfeit of luxury details.

At Harvard's end, turn right (east) onto E. Highland Dr. To your left is the hulking 1910 concrete mansion of Sam Hill, part of the family who owned the Great Northern Railway. He also commissioned the Maryhill Museum and Stonehenge replica in southwest Washington and the Peace Arch at the Canadian border near I-5.

Turn left (north) on 10th Ave. E. To your right is the tasteful brick A-frame structure of Trinity Lutheran Church. A grander religious statement awaits on the left side of 10th. It's the Holy Box (as some call the building) of ❷ **St. Mark's Episcopal Cathedral**. It was designed in 1930 as a neo-Byzantine palace of worship, but Depression-era finances left it unfinished, particularly on the outside. Some brick cladding was finally stuck onto the front decades later; it's now finally being completed. Behind the building, a preserved greenbelt with a privately maintained garden extends down The Hill's northwest slope. To its north, the Gage Academy of Art occupies a former girls' school that was later part of Cornish College of the Arts (Walk 8).

Turn right (east) on E. Galer St. In 1910 Henry Kleinberg, a successful hay merchant, built the elaborate stucco mansion on your right. It was up for sale in 2010 for a mere $4.8 million. KING-TV founder Dorothy Bullitt once owned the brick Tudor mansion to your left.

Turn right (south) on Federal Ave. E. and go four blocks. Most of the homes here are of more modest, upper-middle-class size but still handsome and well kept. It's hard to believe much of Capitol Hill was once in steep decline. In the 1970s the Boeing Bust recession combined with white flight and suburbanization to send neighborhood housing prices into a tailspin. They soared back and then some in the 1990s and 2000s, then dipped a little again.

Turn right (west) on E. Roy St., between two more classic Anhalt apartment buildings. In the 1980s the building on the south side was the fictional home of comic book hero Green Arrow. Continue as Roy bends southwest to Broadway E.

On the south side of Roy is the DeLuxe Bar & Grill, a neighborhood hangout since the 1930s. To its west, the stately Women's Century Club later housed the Harvard Exit art-house cinema; it's now offices. Across Roy from that is a Daughters of the American Revolution chapter, designed as a small-scale replica of George Washington's Mount Vernon, New York, home. East of that is the Loveless Building, a 1930 apartment-retail structure. It's another Tudor Revival affair, complete with a central courtyard. One tenant, the Cook Weaver restaurant, has an elaborate mural depicting a Pushkin fairy tale. It's left over from the Russian restaurant originally in that space.

Return to the east side of Broadway and go right (south). Two blocks (and two block-long mixed-use megaprojects) later, ❸ **All Pilgrims Christian Church** is a century-old brick edifice with great acoustics inside and a gay-friendly rainbow flag outside.

Continue south through the Broadway retail strip. Here are trendy bistros (Julia's), affordable ethnic meals (Jai Thai, Pho Cyclo), espresso joints (Vivace), clothes (Panache, Mishu), and much more. Kitty-corner from All Pilgrims is the Broadway Market building. The 1989 complex preserves the name, and the brick and terra-cotta facade, of a 1928 minimall. There's another false front at Broadway and E. Olive Way, where a Rite Aid pharmacy sits behind the old Broadway Theater's marquee. Halfway down the next block is another Dick's Drive-In. Its walk-up windows host an ever-changing human parade. Across Broadway from Dick's, the light-rail ❹ **Capitol Hill Station** has a big public art mural by local cartoonist Ellen Forney.

Turn right (west) on Olive, which soon curves southwest. Here are more cool eateries (Glo's, Dino's Tomato Pie), bars (Stumbling Monk, Captain Black's, Revolver), shops (including the ❺ **Pretty Parlor** retro-fashion boutique), and art spaces. At Olive and Bellevue Ave. E., ❻ **City Market** is an indie deli-mart with cute cartoon sandwich signs in front, often in the form of ersatz celebrity endorsements.

From here you can backtrack to Olive and Howell, and catch a 14 bus to your starting point. Or you can backtrack a little farther to Olive and Summit, then walk five blocks left (north) back to Mercer.

This walk connects easily to four other walks. From St. Mark's you can take a steep downhill trail to Walk 27. At Federal and E. Aloha St. you're four blocks west of Walk 11. At Federal and 10th you're 0.75 mile south of Walk 27. At E. Olive Way and E. Denny Way you're three steep downhill blocks east of Walk 8. This walk ends two blocks north of Walk 5.

Anhalt Apartments

West Capitol Hill and Broadway

Points of Interest

1 **Top Pot Doughnuts** 609 Summit Ave. E., 206-323-7841, toppotdoughnuts.com

2 **St. Mark's Episcopal Cathedral** 1245 10th Ave. E., 206-323-0300, saintmarks.org

3 **All Pilgrims Christian Church** 500 Broadway E., 206-322-0487, allpilgrims.org

4 **Capitol Hill Station** 140 Broadway E., soundtransit.org

5 **Pretty Parlor** 119 Summit Ave. E., 206-405-2883, prettyparlor.com

6 **City Market** 1722 Bellevue Ave., 206-323-1715

11 East Capitol Hill
Mansions and Monuments

Above: *Volunteer Park water tower*

BOUNDARIES: 13th Ave. E., E. Olive St., 16th Ave. E., and E. Howe St.
DISTANCE: 2.75 miles
DIFFICULTY: Easy (almost all flat)
PARKING: Free street parking
PUBLIC TRANSIT: Metro route 10 stops near this walk's start.

Seattle used to be promoted as having "seven hills," just like Rome. We lost one of those to the Denny Regrade (Walk 7). Of the remaining slopes, only one is known simply as The Hill. It's Capitol Hill, rising just east of downtown. For decades it was Seattle's densest neighborhood, before all the Belltown and South Lake Union condo towers went up. It's still a hearty mélange of artists, students, LGBTQ folks, families, and people of many subcultures and ethnicities. Our next three walks traverse different portions of The Hill. This particular walk takes you to its summit and includes a regal cemetery, a palatial greenhouse, an Art Deco museum housing Asian art, some huge old mansions, and some solid old middle-class homes and apartments.

Walk Description

Start on 15th Ave. E. and E. Garfield St., at Louisa Boren Park. It's a tall bluff above, and connected to, Interlaken Park (Walk 27). From here you can also see Lake Washington, the Cascade mountains, and Bellevue. Turn south onto 15th, then walk briefly southeast to the entrance of ❶ **Lake View Cemetery,** which holds the remains of some of Seattle's founding families (some of whom were moved up to three times as early burial lands were redeveloped).

Take a clockwise loop through the cemetery's paved paths, as follows:

Go straight from the entrance until the path bends left.

Take the first right. As this path curves south, to your right you see the elaborate monument to sawmill baron Henry Yesler, his wife, and an unnamed third person (rumored to be the female lover of either or both Yeslers). Just beyond that is the far plainer gravestone of Princess Angeline, daughter of Chief Sealth (for whom Seattle is named).

Saint Nicholas Russian Orthodox Cathedral, built in 1937

Follow this curving perimeter path around the property's west and then north sides. Elaborate Victorian monuments bear family names you've already seen on your walks—Chittenden, Mercer, Bell, Stone, Nordstrom—while smaller markers remember hundreds of the more obscure. This path curves south near the Nisei War Memorial Monument honoring Japanese Americans who died in World War II.

Turn right at a four-way crossroads, and then turn left. Winding southeast from a mausoleum, you will find the Denny family's quite elaborate monument.

Across the road from that are Lake View's most famous graves, those of actor Bruce Lee and his son Brandon. Due south of there, a big sequoia tree stands above the very modest grave markers of David "Doc" Maynard and his wife, Catherine (Walk 15).

Take two left turns and one right turn, back to the entrance gate and to 15th.

Turn right (south) on 15th, which at this point has a sidewalk only on its east side. Cross back to the west side at the intersection with E. Galer St., which becomes E. Highland Dr. as it enters Volunteer Park.

Turn right and walk southwest on Highland past a kids' play area, toward the statue of Alaska Purchase instigator William Seward. Behind that is the ❷ **Volunteer Park Conservatory**, a Victorian greenhouse styled after London's Crystal Palace. Its five main rooms house cacti, ferns, palms, bromeliads (members of the pineapple family), a corpse flower (which blooms only rarely—and is mightily stinky when it does), and seasonally rotated plant displays.

Graves of Bruce and Brandon Lee at Lake View Cemetery

Turn left (south) from the statue on Volunteer Park Rd. To your left is the ❸ **Seattle Asian Art Museum,** whose 1933 Art Moderne building is as beautiful as any of the works within it. (It's closed at press time for enlarging; it's scheduled to reopen in early 2019.) To your right, Isamu Noguchi's circular sculpture *Black Sun* (inspiration for the Soundgarden song title) frames a Space Needle view, with a large reservoir in between. Ahead of you is a 75-foot-tall water tower. If you climb its 106 steps, you reach an observation deck with great views and educational posters about the Olmsted Brothers' park plan.

From the tower's south side, leave the park heading south on 14th Ave. E. You're on Millionaires' Row, a largely intact strip of opulent, large early-20th-century homes. One of them, the ❹ **Shafer Baillie Mansion** at 14th and Aloha, is now a bed-and-breakfast.

Turn east on E. Roy St., the old southern end to Millionaires' Row. (Its homeowners once had a gate installed here, even though it's a public street.) When you're back at 15th, turn right. This is more typical Capitol Hill housing stock—some classic box houses, some Craftsman bungalows, and some early- to mid-20th-century apartments.

South of E. Mercer St. are the quasi-Tudor Fredonia Apartments, with the recently upscaled ❺ **Canterbury Ale House** on the ground floor. This is the start of the 15th Ave. business strip. These four packed blocks mix the basics (a drugstore and a dry cleaner) with gift boutiques,

Backstory: The Olmsted Plan

In 1903, Seattle hired the Massachusetts-based Olmsted Brothers design firm to devise a master plan for the city's park system. The Olmsteds (whose father, Frederick Law Olmsted, had designed New York City's Central Park) came up with a scheme to place a park or playground within 0.5 mile of every home in town, connected by 20 miles of broad boulevards with wide green median strips. Led by John Charles and Frederick Law Jr., the Olmsted firm continued to consult on Seattle's open spaces for the next three decades.

coffeehouses, and many kinds of bars and restaurants. Of particular note are ❻ **European Vine Selections** (a wine shop with a plain storefront and a huge selection), Coastal Kitchen (an upscale fish house), and ❼ **Victrola Coffee Roasters** (a coffeehouse always packed with local characters).

Turn left (east) on E. Thomas St. for one block. To its south is the former main campus of Group Health Cooperative, founded in 1947 as a patient-owned health care provider. Today it's part of the Kaiser Permanente group and is one of the big five Pill Hill medical complexes on Capitol and First Hills.

Turn right (south) on 16th Ave. E. and go three blocks, past modest prewar homes and classic brick apartments. At the corner with E. John St., a distinguished-looking former Methodist church now houses an Internet marketing firm. A block away at E. Denny Way, an equally handsome former Christian Science church has been divided into condos.

Head right (west) three blocks on E. Howell St. At 15th, the Gaslight Inn B&B occupies a particularly fancy old bungalow. At 13th is the 1960s Greek Orthodox Church of the Assumption. The clean, white structure topped by a modern, modest dome is best seen from the back.

Turn left (south) and go one block on 13th to view the smaller but much more elaborate ❽ **Saint Nicholas Russian Orthodox Cathedral**. Its roof features three golden onion domes surrounding a six-sided spire. On the block's end at E. Olive St. is the former Advent Christian Church, a solid brick box.

From here you can return east to 15th or continue south one more block to E. Pine St. Either option will lead to a 10 bus heading back to your start.

This walk connects easily to two other walks. At 13th and Aloha you're three blocks east of Walk 10. This route ends one block north of Walk 5.

Points of Interest

1 **Lake View Cemetery** 1554 15th Ave. E., 206-322-1582, lakeviewcemeteryassociation.com

2 **Volunteer Park Conservatory** 1402 E. Galer St., 206-684-4743, volunteerparkconservatory.org

3 **Seattle Asian Art Museum** 1400 E. Prospect St., 206-654-3100, seattleartmuseum.org

4 **Shafer Baillie Mansion** 907 14th Ave. E., 206-322-4654, sbmansion.com

5 **Canterbury Ale House** 534 15th Ave. E., 206-325-3110, thecanterburyalehouse.com

6 **European Vine Selections** 522 15th Ave E., 206-323-3557, evswines.com

7 **Victrola Coffee Roasters** 411 15th Ave. E., 206-325-6520, victrolacoffee.com

8 **Saint Nicholas Russian Orthodox Cathedral** 1714 13th Ave. E., 206-905-9636, saintnicholascathedral.org

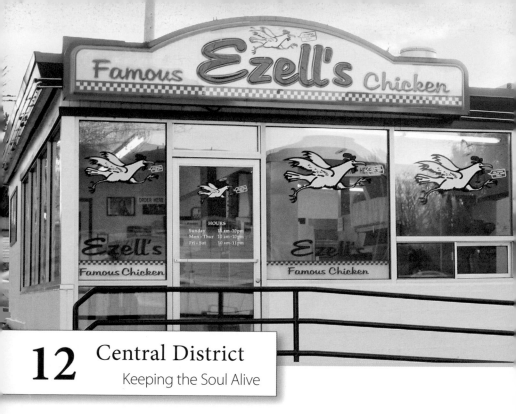

12 Central District
Keeping the Soul Alive

Above: Ezell's was endorsed by Oprah Winfrey.

BOUNDARIES: 23rd Ave., E. Jackson St., 14th Ave., and E. Union St.
DISTANCE: 3 miles
DIFFICULTY: Moderate (mostly flat or downhill)
PARKING: Free and metered street parking
PUBLIC TRANSIT: Metro routes 3 and 4 stop at this walk's start.

This valley neighborhood, with no scenic views, was one of the few sections of Seattle where African Americans could own homes before the 1950s. It's still the spiritual center of the city's black community, even after the current real estate boom displaced many longtime residents in favor of more upscale arrivistes. You'll see more humbly sized, albeit handsomely preserved (in many cases), homes than in some of this book's other walks. The Central District also has its share of big institutional structures, including a theater in a former Jewish temple, another theater in a former Scandinavian community center, and a stoic brick hospital.

Walk Description

Start on the north side of E. Jefferson St., walking east from 17th Ave. You're in front of ❶ **Swedish Medical Center: Cherry Hill Campus**. The spire and neon cross atop this stately brick castle of medicine are left over from its original operators, the Sisters of Providence (the two organizations have since merged). A hospital-wide PA system used to play harp music to denote each newborn baby.

Turn left (north) on 18th Ave., initially along the hospital's back. At 18th and Columbia St. there's a tiny, plain, white-paneled storefront church. On the next block is a more elaborate monument to faith, ❷ **Immaculate Conception Catholic Church**. The 1904 brick edifice is a mix of Romanesque, Baroque, and Byzantine design schticks and features twin bell towers. Its many interior embellishments include a two-thirds-scale replica of France's Our Lady of Lourdes Grotto.

Across from T. T. Minor grade school at 18th and Union St. is a little strip of storefronts, including the Gallery 1412 art and performance space. Turning right (east) on the north side of Union, you soon reach ❸ **Central Cinema**, known for very eclectic programming. (Alongside artier fare, they once screened a Worst of Madonna film series.)

Turn right (south) on 23rd Ave. past blocks of solid old homes, some of them recently remodeled with varying results. To your left, south of E. Cherry St., is the sloped concrete facade of the Medgar Evers Pool, a public facility named for the Mississippi Civil Rights martyr. To your right, at E. Jefferson St., is ❹ **Ezell's,** a tiny fried-chicken joint that counts Oprah Winfrey among its fans. As you cross Jefferson, glance east to see the ex–Providence Hospital spire.

Continue south on 23rd, heading slightly uphill. On your left, south of Jefferson, Garfield High School is a restored 1920s brick and terra-cotta masterpiece. Its high-profile alums include musicians Quincy Jones and Jimi Hendrix. At Yesler Way, the ❺ **Douglass-Truth Library** is a gracious old building (renamed in recent years after emancipation advocates Frederick Douglass and Sojourner Truth) combined with a sleek, metal-clad new building. Kitty-corner from there, the Art Deco former Fire Station 6 features relief art of lightning bolts above its doors, symbolizing the then new (1931) tool of radio dispatch. A pair of strip malls, including a jazz-nostalgia-themed Starbucks, stands at S. Jackson St.; they're set to be redeveloped.

Turn right (west) on Jackson. You soon pass Washington Middle School, the Washington Vocational Institute, the giant Franz Bakery plant (its thrift store is a great spot for a midwalk snack), several affordable Asian eateries, and, on a good day, a peek of Mount Rainier to the southeast. At 18th Ave. S., the new Legacy Pratt Park apartment complex bears the restored rooftop sign of the block's former occupant, Wonder Bread. The bakery is gone, but the sign still leads motorists toward one of Seattle's least white-bread neighborhoods.

Backtrack one block to 19th and Jackson; turn left (north). At 19th and S. Main St., the ❻ **Pratt Fine Arts Center** offers classes in sculpture, glass art, jewelry, and 2-D art. Tours are available by appointment. Continue north, into and through Edwin T. Pratt Park, to E. Yesler Way.

Turn left (west) on Yesler. At 17th Ave., the ❼ **Langston Hughes Performing Arts Institute** has held theater, dance, film, and other events since 1969 in a majestic former synagogue. Appropriately, B. Marcus Priteca, Seattle's foremost theater architect, designed the building in 1913.

Turn right (north) on 14th Ave. at the old St. George Hotel. This stately Victorian brick edifice, with elegant brick and stone cladding, was built in 1910 as a residential hotel catering to Asian immigrants. It now houses the ❽ **Urban League of Metropolitan Seattle**. One block away at E. Fir St., ❾ **Washington Hall** was originally a 1908 Danish Brotherhood settlement house. It became a jazz venue in the 1940s, an African American Masonic lodge in the 1970s, and the original On the Boards performance space (Walk 18) in the 1980s. It still hosts theater and dance shows, under the management of preservation group Historic Seattle. Across 14th, the Squire Park P-Patch features art panels by artist Mary Coss alongside the community garden plots.

Continue on 14th for four blocks. To your left, north of Spruce St., the King County Youth Center's public art (a tile mural, a whale-fin sculpture) fails to negate the sprawling, decaying 1960s social-service complex's impersonal presence. A more human-scale presence awaits at 13th Ave. and Jefferson St. in the form of Nate's Wings and Waffles.

This walk connects easily to two walks. It ends two blocks east and three blocks south of Walk 6. At 18th and Jackson you're six blocks east of Walk 13.

Washington Hall's restored brick front

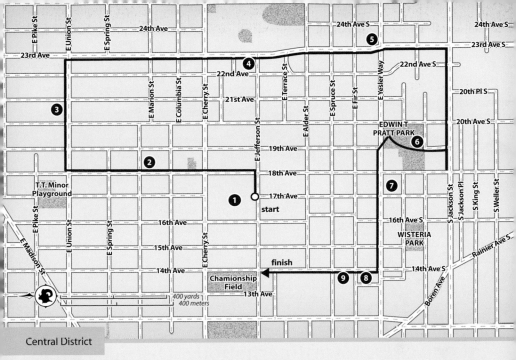

Points of Interest

1. **Swedish Medical Center: Cherry Hill Campus** 500 17th Ave., 206-320-2000, swedish.org

2. **Immaculate Conception Church** 820 18th Ave., 206-322-5970, icseattle.org

3. **Central Cinema** 1411 21st Ave., 206-328-2320, central-cinema.com

4. **Ezell's Famous Chicken** 501 23rd Ave., 206-324-4141, ezellschicken.com

5. **Douglass-Truth Library** 2300 E. Yesler Way, 206-684-4704, spl.org/locations/douglass-truth-branch

6. **Pratt Fine Arts Center** 1902 S. Main St., 206-328-2200, pratt.org

7. **Langston Hughes Performing Arts Institute** 104 17th Ave. S., 206-323-7067, langstonseattle.org

8. **Urban League of Metropolitan Seattle** 105 14th Ave., 206-461-3792, urbanleague.org

9. **Washington Hall** 153 14th Ave., 206-322-1511, washingtonhall.org

13 Chinatown-International District
A Taste of the East

Above: Mongolian Hot Pot, one of many Asian dining choices on this walk

BOUNDARIES: 5th Ave. S., 12th Ave. S., S. Main St., and S. Vermont St.
DISTANCE: 1.75 miles
DIFFICULTY: Easy (1 brief incline)
PARKING: Limited metered street parking; pay lots and garages include the Uwajimaya Village lot at 600 5th Ave. S.
PUBLIC TRANSIT: Seattle Transit Tunnel International District Station; the First Hill Streetcar and a dozen Metro routes stop at or near 5th Ave. S. and S. Jackson St.

This region would not be what it is without the vital contributions of Chinese American railway workers, Japanese American farmers, and Filipino American cannery workers—contributions that have not always been appreciated. White militants in 1886 staged anti-Chinese riots, rounding up 350 people and ordering them at gunpoint to board the next steamship out of town. During World War II, Japanese Americans throughout the Pacific states were sent to internment camps. Through it all, the neighborhood east of Pioneer Square has remained the spiritual home of Asian Seattle. In recent decades, Vietnamese immigrants have added their own dimensions to this exciting mélange of languages, architectures, and decorative styles. Yet even this historic area is not immune to redevelopment mania. New apartment and hotel projects are planned for its periphery, and even for current historic-building spots in its heart.

Walk Description

Start outside the Transit Tunnel's International District Station at 5th Ave. S. and S. King St. To your west is neoclassical Union Station, the larger of Seattle's two heritage railway stations. Its restored lobby is a rental party space.

South of Union Station, Paul Allen has built four neomodern midrise buildings. If you didn't know about Allen's sci-fi appreciation (he named his company Vulcan), you can tell by the big air vents at 5th and Weller, between two of Allen's buildings. They look like abstracted versions of *Doctor Who*'s archvillains, the Daleks.

Cross 5th Ave. S. As you reach King St., walk under an elaborate 45-foot Chinese archway built in 2008. Walk east along King St. one block to 6th Ave. S. At the northeast corner, a hostel occupies the 1925 American Hotel. At the southeast corner, the Pink Gorilla store offers vintage video games.

Turn left (north) on 6th and continue for two blocks. At 6th and S. Jackson St., a branch of Washington Federal Savings sports a mansard roof with Chinese-inspired red tile; its front sports a mural portrait of eight Chinese "immortals."

Across Jackson, the Higo five-and-ten store is now ❶ **Kobo,** a crafts gallery and home-furnishings store. North of Jackson, the 1903 Main Street School Annex was Seattle's first kinder-garten; the small wood-frame building is now offices. It's across from the 1914 NP Hotel, now low-income apartments.

Turn right (east) onto S. Main St. at a neon rice bowl outside a now-closed café. This seg-ment goes steeply uphill but only for a block. Halfway up, the 1910 ❷ **Panama Hotel** contains a tea and coffee house and a private museum (open by appointment) remembering the Japanese American community before the World War II internment. Across the street, ❸ **Kobe Terrace Park** includes a community garden rising up a hillside, with a 200-year-old stone lantern at its top.

Turn right (south) on Maynard Ave. S. back to Jackson. The Far East Building shows the result of a 1908 street regrade; what are now its street-level storefronts were built beneath what had been two separate buildings. At the southwest corner, the 1915 Bush Hotel now has four floors of low-income apartments above two floors of retail and community-organization offices.

Turn left (east) on Jackson. At Maynard Ave. S., *Heaven, Man, and Earth* is a 12-foot abstract bronze sculpture by local artist George Tsutakawa. East of that, Asia Bar-B-Que entices with roasted chickens hanging in the window. Just south of the southwest corner of Jackson and 7th Ave. S., ❹ **Theatre Off Jackson** stages plays and screens films in a 1915-era garage.

Continue along the north side of Jackson under the I-5 freeway overpass pillars, painted red and gold with Native American fish icons. Just beyond the freeway is the Pacific Rim Center, a condo-retail box anchored by the Joyale Seafood Restaurant.

Continue toward 12th Ave. S., now the main drag of Seattle's Vietnamese community. It used to be the center of a thriving jazz scene, centered in bars and private after-hours clubs. This history is noted in a small freestanding plaque near 12th and Jackson's northwest corner.

Turn right (south) on 12th. Turn right (west) on King, through a largely industrial block. At 10th Ave. S., the King Street Southern Baptist Church and Chinese Southern Baptist Mission is a small, solid redbrick box with Gothic stained glass windows.

Continue along King under the freeway pillars, with King Street Station's clock tower (Walk 1) in front of you. At 8th and King, the 1910 East Kong Yick Building houses the ❺ **Wing Luke Asian Museum,** which calls itself the only "pan-Asian Pacific American museum" in the United States. Across King, the Bing Kung Association (a tong, or fraternal organization aiding immigrants) features a tiled balcony on its fourth floor, with a Masonic logo in relief above it. (The building once housed a Masonic temple.)

On the south side of King between 7th Ave. S. and Maynard Ave. is Maynard Alley. It includes the now-razed former site of Wah Mee, a private gambling club dating to the 1920s. In 1983 it was the site of Washington State's worst mass murder when three robbers shot 14 people, killing all but one.

At King and Maynard Ave., the 1909 Rex Hotel houses ❻ **Tai Tung,** the neighborhood's oldest continuously operating restaurant (since 1935). It's kitty-corner from the recently enlarged ❼ **Hing Hay Park,** with an elaborate multicultural mural and a grand Chinese pavilion (made in Taiwan).

Turn left (south) on Maynard. Just south of King, a round window with red and black brick "sunbeams" marks the Eastern Hotel. It was built in 1911 by a company founded in 1868 by Chin Chun Hock, probably Seattle's first Chinese settler. It now has a minimuseum honoring Filipino writer Carlos Bulosan, who once lived here. It also houses the ❽ **Seattle Pinball Museum,** a storefront filled with restored American flipper games. For a $7.50 admission fee, you can play for as long as you can stand the noise.

Just south of the Eastern is the Sing Keong Society (another Chinese benevolent association), with a pagoda-style false front. South of S. Weller St., observe the ❾ **Bush Garden** karaoke bar's simple stone-and-bamboo facade. It's more exquisite on the inside.

Backtrack half a block to Maynard and Weller. Turn left (west) on Weller and walk one block, past the Mongolian Hot Pot restaurant's elaborate storefront. At 6th and Weller, Oasis Tea Zone and a private event space occupy part of the blue-tile-roofed former home of the Uwajimaya Asian grocery store. It currently anchors ❿ **Uwajimaya Village,** across Weller to your left. Enter and view the shops at the complex's north side, starting with the Kinokuniya Bookstore, a Japanese chain. It has many beautiful gift items even if you don't read the language. Head out the bookstore's south doors into a mall area, then into the Uwajimaya store itself. It offers food, fashions, home decor, cookware, toys, and gifts. Exit through the store's south entrance, and turn left (east) back to 6th Ave. S. at S. Lane St.

Turn right (south) on 6th Ave. On the east side, a new low-rise commercial building includes Daiso, the Japanese equivalent of a dollar store (most items here range from $1.50 to $2). You reach the end of 6th at a diagonal intersection with Seattle Blvd. S., in front of the former U.S. Immigrant Station and Assay Office. Thousands of new citizens came through this neoclassical edifice from 1932 to 2004. Some stayed for weeks or months, jailed under the Chinese Exclusion Act (effective 1882–1943) before they could join relatives already living in the United States. The 77,000-square-foot building reopened in 2010 as ⓫ **Inscape,** a complex of artist studios and exhibit spaces.

Cross Seattle Blvd. and turn left (southeast). The boxy modern building next to the former immigration complex houses Glass Box Gallery, an art installation space.

Take a dogleg right turn back onto 6th and walk one block, to the large brick warehouse at S. Vermont St. At that building's left end is ⓬ **Big John's PFI** (also known as Pacific Food Importers), a bulk-foods outlet with European cheeses, meats, olive oils, and pasta.

Backtrack to Seattle Blvd., walk northwest to 5th, and turn north to return to your start.

This walk connects easily to four other walks. It starts one block south and three blocks east of Walk 1, and eight blocks from Walk 4. It ends one block north and five blocks east of Walk 14. At 12th and Jackson you're six blocks west of Walk 12.

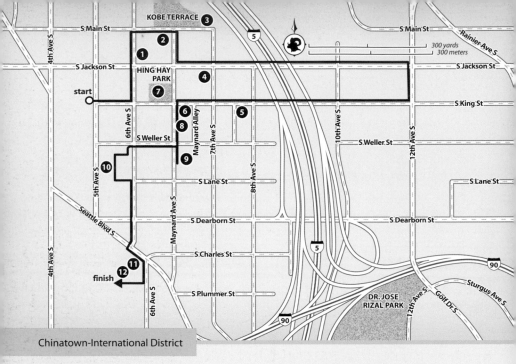

Chinatown-International District

Points of Interest

① Kobo at Higo 604 S. Jackson St., 206-381-3000, koboseattle.com

② Panama Hotel Tea & Coffee House 607 S. Main St., 206-515-4000, panamahotel.net

③ Kobe Terrace Park 650 S. Main St., seattle.gov/parks/find/parks/kobe-terrace

④ Theatre Off Jackson 409 7th Ave. S., 206-340-1049, theatreoffjackson.org

⑤ Wing Luke Asian Museum 719 S. King St., 206-623-5124, wingluke.org

⑥ Tai Tung 659 S. King St., 206-622-7372, taitungrestaurant.com

⑦ Hing Hay Park 423 Maynard Ave. S., 206-684-4075, seattle.gov/parks/find/parks/hing-hay-park

⑧ Seattle Pinball Museum 508 Maynard Ave. S., 206-623-0759, seattlepinballmuseum.com

⑨ Bush Garden 614 Maynard Ave. S., 206-682-6830, bushgarden.net

⑩ Uwajimaya 600 5th Ave. S., 206-624-6248, uwajimaya.com

⑪ Inscape 815 Seattle Blvd. S., 206-458-2716, inscapearts.org

⑫ Big John's PFI 1001 6th Ave. S., 206-682-2022, bigjohnspfiseattle.com

14 SoDo Industrial District
Sports Fans and Factories

BOUNDARIES: S. Royal Brougham Way, 4th Ave. S., Chelan Ave. SW, and SW Spokane St.
DISTANCE: 4 miles, in 2 segments
DIFFICULTY: Easy (almost entirely flat)
PARKING: Pay lots and garages include the official Safeco Field and CenturyLink Field garages, which are emptier on non-game days.
PUBLIC TRANSIT: Link light-rail Stadium Station; many Metro routes stop along 4th Ave. S. and the SoDo Busway

"TIDE LANDS HAS BIZ!" Early Seattle real estate speculator H. H. Richardson chanted and printed that slogan to promote land sales in the then-underwater lands south of Pioneer Square. He meant these properties were rising in value, because they would eventually rise above sea level. Richardson's prophecies proved correct when dirt from the Denny Regrade (Walk 7) and other projects turned these wetlands high, dry, and ready for industry. Later promoters christened the area SoDo, for "south of the Kingdome." After there was no more Kingdome, the acronym's meaning was changed to "south of downtown." City zoning regulations, intended to preserve industrial businesses and their living-wage jobs, have mostly protected this bastion of working-class values from redevelopment. Along these wide, flat avenues you'll see a variety of structures made for the making and storing of a variety of things. The structures range from the new and functional to the weathered and gorgeous.

Walk Description

Start at the northwest entrance to ❶ **Safeco Field,** on the east side of 1st Ave. S. south of S. Royal Brougham Way. The older of the Kingdome's two replacement stadia, it's been home to the Mariners baseball team since 1999. Even when the team's not so hot, the stadium (with its high-tech retractable roof) is one of baseball's snazziest. Across 1st, the Pyramid Alehouse is the showcase pub for one of the region's biggest specialty brewers. (Royal Brougham Way was originally Connecticut St. In the 1980s it was rechristened in honor of a *Post-Intelligencer* sportswriter who died with his figurative boots on, in the Kingdome press box during a Seahawks football game.)

Walk south, past Safeco Field's even grander southwest entrance at 1st and Edgar Martinez Dr. S. (a single block of S. Atlantic St., renamed for the Mariners' former designated hitter). On the following block, a tall, narrow, handsome old brick industrial building stands watch over a block that's largely been razed for surface parking lots. Across from that, a modern office complex includes the downsized studios of KING, the Northwest's oldest TV station.

Orient Express restaurant (formerly Andy's Diner)

South of S. Massachusetts St. are the Showbox SoDo music club and a wine shop in a former Murphy bed factory. South of the latter is Hooverville Bar, named for the Depression-era shanty-town that was near here. Beyond S. Holgate St., a huge and usually empty Krispy Kreme snack shop stands as an icon of yesterday's next big thing. South of that stands the gallery of wildlife and nature photographer Art Wolfe.

South of S. Walker St., a white warehouse building houses Outdoor Research, selling serious camping and hiking clothes and gear. At S. Stacy St., artifacts at the ❷ **Living Computers Museum + Labs** (another Paul Allen–funded gift to the city) include the old IBM mainframe seen on TV's *Mad Men*. Across from that, a onetime gas station is the ❸ **Pecos Pit BBQ** stand, a sandwich shop with no indoor seating (just a couple of picnic tables outside) and sometimes-huge lines for its tender meats smothered in sauce. Down the next block is a popular Vietnamese café, Pho Cyclo.

Looking west, spy the green eyes of a cartoon mermaid peering from a 1907 brick clock tower. Cross to the west side of 1st for a closer look at Starbucks Center, the coffee giant's world headquarters. Seattle's largest commercial building by square footage, it was originally a Sears catalog warehouse. In 1925, the then catalog-only company built its second-ever retail store on the building's south side (it closed in 2014). Appropriately, a building made for yesterday's top shop-at-home company is now partly occupied by today's top shop-at-home company, with an Amazon Fresh Grocery pick-up station.

At S. Hanford St., you have lovingly restored mid-century kitsch at the K. R. Trigger and Vertigo buildings. Dentist and developer Scott Andrews bought these warehouses in the 1990s. The latter now houses one of the neighborhood's many legal pot stores. Cross 1st at the south side of Hanford, toward two more Andrews-developed wooden buildings. One of these, Sodo Park, is a rental reception space.

Backtrack north along the east side of 1st. South of S. Forest St., ❹ **Silver Platters** has Seattle's largest selection of new and used CDs and vinyl records, plus DVDs (remember those?). Just across Forest is an example of Seattle-First National Bank's handsome old branch design, which Bank of America still occupies. At the southeast corner of 1st and Lander, peer in at vintage signs at Western Neon. At the northeast corner with Lander, a classic wooden-barn-style warehouse has housed a series of home-furnishings stores for more than six decades; its current tenant is Pius Kitchen & Bath.

Turn right (east) on Lander, toward 4th Ave. S. On Lander's south side, ❺ **Pacific Galleries** operates a huge antique mall and auction house.

Turn right (south) on the east side of 4th. The first building you encounter is the Art Deco yet utilitarian quarters of Esquin Wine Merchants. At 4th and Forest, across from Seattle's last Denny's franchise, the always-joyful pink neon of an Elephant Car Wash (Walk 7) stands adjacent to the

Rabanco Recycling plant's loading platform. There, you can see huge piles of printed matter go to the great beyond.

❻ Orient Express, at 4th and Hanford, is a Chinese restaurant and lounge in a collection of old passenger railcars previously known for decades as Andy's Diner. Across from it is a colorful new branch of Pick-Quick, a burger chain founded in Tacoma's suburbs. The Spanish suburban–style Fire Station 14, with two firefighter-training towers in back, has stood guard at 4th and Hanford since 1927.

On the west side of 4th, south of S. Spokane St., view the giant white and pink neon City Light letters on an electric substation. You could end your walk here, taking a Metro bus at the northeast corner of 4th and Spokane back to Safeco Field. Or you could continue south on 4th another 0.4 mile, past the substation's lovely lattice towers, to **❼ Costco Wholesale**'s original megastore.

If you're continuing with this walk, backtrack to 4th and Spokane. Turn left (west) onto the north side of Spokane. Be warned: This sidewalk, in the shadow of an auto-only viaduct and lined with rental-truck lots and loading docks, is lonely.

That all changes once you're west of East Marginal Way S. Here, you get a wide pedestrian and bicycle path separated from the roadway and lined with grass and occasional trees. As it crosses the Duwamish Waterway's east fork, it offers a sequence of three sheltered viewpoints looking out to the harbor. (You can fish here; just don't eat your catch.) This path leads onto Harbor Island, built for industry in 1909 from fill dirt poured into the Duwamish delta. It's now mostly container docks, but you can still see the former Dutch Boy paint plant (now run by a Japanese firm) and the mammoth grain elevators of the defunct Fisher Flouring Mill.

While you're on Harbor Island, cross SW Spokane St. at the first available crosswalk at the intersection with SW Manning St. Enter the pedestrian and bicycle lane on Spokane's south side. This will get you across the (lower) West Seattle Bridge, across the Duwamish's west fork.

Once you're back on land, follow the ALKI TRAIL signs on the path as it turns northwest from Spokane to SW Marginal Pl., then cross three short crosswalks onto Chelan Ave. SW, north of Spokane. Your reward for a well-trod walk is a bite and/or sip at the **❽ Chelan Cafe,** a venerable working folks' lunch spot. Just west of there, another trio of crosswalks gets you to a bus stop. Take route 21, 22, or 56 back to your start.

This walk connects easily to three other walks. It starts one long block south of Walk 1, and it ends at the same place as Walk 34. Following the Alki Trail past this walk's end will get you (after 1.75 miles) to Walk 15.

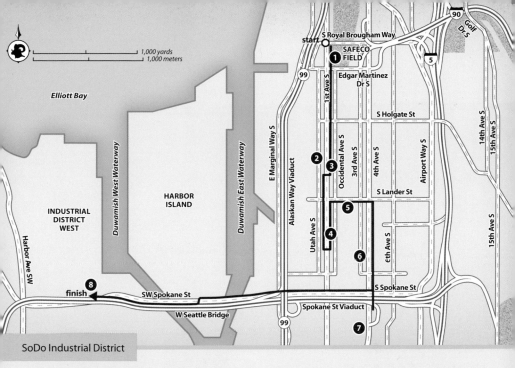

Points of Interest

① **Safeco Field** 1250 1st Ave. S., 206-346-4001, mariners.com

② **Living Computers Museum + Labs** 2245 1st Ave. S., 206-342-2020, livingcomputers.org

③ **Pecos Pit BBQ** 2260 1st Ave. S., 206-623-0629, pecospit.com

④ **Silver Platters** 2930 1st Ave. S., 206-283-3472, silverplatters.com

⑤ **Pacific Galleries** 241 S. Lander St., 206-292-3999, pacgal.com

⑥ **Orient Express** 2963 4th Ave. S., 206-682-0683, seattleorientexpress.com

⑦ **Costco Wholesale** 4401 4th Ave. S., 206-622-3136, costco.com

⑧ **Chelan Cafe** 3527 Chelan Ave. SW, 206-932-7383

15 Alki
A Birthplace at a Beach

Above: *Seacrest Park, where the water taxi docks*

BOUNDARIES: Harbor Ave. SW, California Way SW, foot of Alki Ave. SW
DISTANCE: 3.25 miles
DIFFICULTY: Easy (all flat, mostly on pedestrian/bicycle paths)
PARKING: Free but scarce street parking near Seacrest Park
PUBLIC TRANSIT: King County Water Taxi from the downtown waterfront or Metro routes 37, 773, and 775

On a miserable November day in 1851, 10 adults and 12 children landed in a schooner on a windswept beach to meet David Denny, who'd arrived before to scout possible settlement sites. They named their dreary outpost New York–Alki ("New York by-and-by" in Chinook jargon). The following spring, the settlers mostly moved east to today's Pioneer Square. Alki later blossomed into a residential and recreational neighborhood. The city preserved several miles of the Puget

Sound shore for public use. Depending on the season, you could find yourself walking here among hundreds of inline skaters, cyclists, and parents pushing baby strollers, or among just a few die-hard joggers. The walk leads you to Alki Beach, a highly popular site for sea gazing and socializing (and, during the peak years of the hot-rod culture, for car cruising).

Walk Description

Start at ❶ **Seacrest Park,** perhaps by taking the ❷ **King County Water Taxi** from Pier 50 downtown. If you drive, be warned that water taxi commuters often fill street parking. Seacrest's best-known asset is a spectacular view of the downtown skyline, seen in such films as *The Fabulous Baker Boys*. The park also offers a public fishing pier, a boat launch, and one of three locations of Marination restaurant, serving Hawaiian-Korean fusion cuisine.

Turn right (northwest) onto Harbor Ave. SW. Continue as this glorious promenade bends southwest at Duwamish Head, becoming Alki Ave. SW. This is where you'll find the city's monument to Luna Park, an amusement pier that operated from 1912 until an arsonist torched it in 1933. Old photos depict it as a gloriously tacky, Edwardian pleasure spot. As you walk farther, you find more city-installed monuments to Alki's past and to local sea creatures and plants.

Keep going a leisurely 2 miles on the street's west side, which faces an open, public shore. You may be accompanied by many other walkers, strollers, cyclists, and roller skaters. (Icons on the wide sidewalk tell you which lane to stay in to avoid a bicycle and pedestrian pileup.)

Note two types of residential structures along the street's east side: hulking condominiums and quaint little cottages. While the cottages look more rustic and cozy, they were originally just as upscale as the condos—most were built as summer homes for the well-to-do. This stretch is known to some locals as the pipeline, after an old street runoff pipe buried in rock. It's alternately called the junkyard, after decades-old household debris that appears at low tide.

The shorefront park widens into a broad beach. The bluff behind the condos and cottages gives way to a gentler slope. Older apartment buildings appear on the landward side of the street, as does the start of the Alki business district. Among the first businesses you see is Wheel Fun Rentals, a bicycle rental franchise.

Shortly beyond that is the homey ❸ **Pepperdock Restaurant,** a good place for fish-and-chips and burgers. More dining options await down the street, at a full range of price points. The Alki business strip has become a restaurant row, to the exclusion of most other business types (its only supermarket closed in 2002). Its oldest occupant is ❹ **Spud Fish & Chips,** first opened in 1935.

Side Trip: Lincoln Park and Fauntleroy Ferry Terminal

Three miles south of the Alki Lighthouse along Beach Drive SW (or on bus routes 116 and RapidRide C from downtown or the Junction), the 315-acre Lincoln Park is a contemplative spot atop a bluff on a mini peninsula. It offers views of the Olympics, tall madrona and Douglas-fir trees, a forest-themed jungle gym, a trail with exercise stations, and another trail to a driftwood-adorned beach and a heated-saltwater pool. To Lincoln's north along Fauntleroy Way SW stands the Kenney Retirement Home's neocolonial original building. To its south, the Fauntleroy Ferry Terminal can take you to the still-rural Vashon Island or to Southworth on the Kitsap Peninsula.

Back on the beach is **⑤ Alki Beach Park**'s only building, the historic **⑥ Alki Bathhouse**. It's been remodeled to contain a community meeting hall and public art studios.

Farther down the beach is a miniature Statue of Liberty on a lighthouse-shaped pedestal, a 2008 replacement for a statue the Boy Scouts donated in 1952 (it became an instant gathering spot for folks depositing flowers and mementos after 9/11). You can see the previous copy on display at the Log House Museum, mentioned later in this walk.

Turn back, cross Alki Ave. at 61st Ave. SW, turn left, and walk south a half block to the **⑦ Alki Homestead Restaurant,** built in 1903 as the Fir Lodge. The restaurant's been closed since a 2009 fire, but you can still admire its bulky log-cabin structure and its stoic vertical neon sign. (It's currently being restored.)

Farther south on 61st, past SW Stevens St., you find the **⑧ Log House Museum**. It was originally the carriage house for the building now known as the Alki Homestead. It houses neighborhood mementos and exhibits.

Return to Alki Ave. and 61st. Cross the street to return to Alki Beach Park, then continue southwest until you reach the *Birthplace of Seattle*, a white obelisk marking the first white settlement in present-day Seattle on November 13, 1851. It was revised in 2001 to include the female settlers' first names and to recognize the native peoples who were already here. Its base includes a fragment of Plymouth Rock, installed in 1926.

Recross Alki Ave. at 64th Ave. SW. To the south, tucked inconspicuously on this quiet residential street, you'll find Seattle's oldest existing house at 3045 64th. It's a modest brown structure with cedar trim, built circa 1858 for city cofounder Dr. David S. "Doc" Maynard (a legendary character given more to gregariousness and liquor than to monumental architecture). If it doesn't look historic, that's because it has undergone several expansions and face-lifts.

Backtracking to Alki Ave. lets you check out some whimsical apartment structures, including one vaguely shaped like a series of ship's sails. Too bad the recent condo-building craze has included little or none of this architectural creativity.

Another 0.3 mile down Alki Ave., past the end of the public beach, is the stately white **❾ Alki Point Lighthouse**. Built in 1913, it's open for tours on weekend summer afternoons. The rest of the time, you might skip this segment of the walk; there's not even a good spot to look at the lighthouse from the street.

Backtrack to Alki Drive and 61st. From here you can take a shuttle bus back to the Water Taxi or take a 37 bus to the Admiral district (Walk 35) and downtown.

This walk connects easily with five other walks. The Water Taxi brings you to the central Waterfront (Walk 18), which is also near the Pike Place Market (Walk 3), the downtown retail core (Walks 2 and 4), and Pioneer Square (Walk 1).

An anchor marks the spot of the old Luna Park.

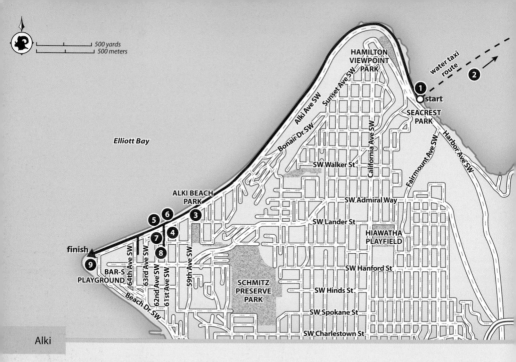

Points of Interest

1 **Seacrest Park** 1660 Harbor Ave. SW, seattle.gov/parks/find/parks/seacrest-park

2 **King County Water Taxi, Pier 50** Alaskan Way and Yesler Way, 206-477-3979, kingcounty.gov /depts/transportation/water-taxi/west-seattle

3 **Pepperdock Restaurant** 2618 Alki Ave. SW, 206-935-1000

4 **Spud Fish & Chips** 2666 Alki Ave. SW, 206-938-0606, alkispud.com

5 **Alki Beach Park** 1702 Alki Ave. SW, seattle.gov/parks/find/parks/alki-beach-park

6 **Alki Bathhouse** 2701 Alki Ave. SW, 206-684-7254, seattle.gov/parks/arts/alkiart.htm

7 **Alki Homestead Restaurant** 2717 61st Ave. SW

8 **Log House Museum** 3003 61st Ave. SW, 206-938-5293, loghousemuseum.info

9 **Alki Point Lighthouse** 3201 Alki Ave. SW, tinyurl.com/alkiptlh

16

Discovery Park to Ballard Locks
Kites, Boats, and Powwows

BOUNDARIES: 36th Ave. W., Discovery Park Blvd., Utah Ave., 32nd Ave. NW, and NW 54th St.
DISTANCE: 5 miles
DIFFICULTY: Difficult (one steep uphill trail)
PARKING: Free parking in Discovery Park east lot, just inside the Government Way entrance
PUBLIC TRANSIT: Metro routes 24 and 33 stop near this walk's start. Routes 17, 29, and 44 stop near its end.

Two of Seattle's most popular scenic spots are legacies from the U.S. Army. The former Fort Lawton in northwest Magnolia, which Seattle gave the Army in 1900 and the Army returned to the city in 1972, is now Discovery Park. The city's biggest park encompasses 534 acres, mostly reclaimed for nature and nature-loving humans. It has walking trails ranging from flat to steep and a restored lighthouse guarding a wide beachfront. Just north of Discovery, the Hiram M. Chittenden (also known as Ballard) Locks, built in 1916 and managed by the Army Corps of

Engineers, is the gateway between Lakes Union and Washington. A key passageway for both pleasure and commercial boats (and for our precious salmon), it also serves as a water-level footbridge across the Lake Washington Ship Canal, with finely landscaped grounds at both ends.

Walk Description

Start at Discovery Park's east entrance, 36th Ave. W. and Discovery Park Blvd. Take the separate sidewalk to the south of the vehicular road.

The first left turn you can take from here leads you, past a parking lot, to the ❶ **Discovery Park Visitor Center**. From there backtrack to, and continue westward on, Discovery Park Blvd., and then turn left onto Washington Ave. This road is initially heavily wooded with mostly deciduous trees. At the top of a mild slope you reach a large clearing.

Washington Ave. heads west, past the Fort Lawton Historic District, two stretches of white-and-yellow painted wood buildings (including officers' residences, a chapel, a bus shelter, and a gym) separated by a huge open meadow (a great place for kite flying and running about). Some of the buildings have been rehabbed as private homes. Amid these old wooden structures sits a piece of Cold War tech, a radar tower shaped like a giant golf ball.

Washington Ave. intersects with Oregon Ave. Turn right (north) on Oregon, as it bends northwest then southwest and intersects with Idaho Ave. Turn right (north) on Idaho toward an old, long bus shelter. (Like many of the old fort structures, it was a location in the 1973 James Caan movie *Cinderella Liberty*.) North of this shelter, turn left on the path that parellels Discovery Park Blvd. It leads initially through a meadow with small trees and shrubs.

Head west on this path as it winds gently downhill, past the old fort stables, then past a 1950s suburban-style military housing tract (which may or may not be still standing as you read this). You might wish to hold your nose as you approach the West Point Treatment Plant. (At least they're scrubbing the city's wastewater now. They used to just pipe it out to sea.)

Past the plant, the air turns to the aroma of salt water as you approach the ❷ **West Point Lighthouse,** still warning ships after 130 years. The city undertook a major restoration of the brick-and-stucco building in 2009–2010. The point itself separates South Beach and North Beach.

Turn east onto North Beach. Turn just inland from the beach onto a main dirt trail that winds between the shore and the treatment plant's north wall, which is mostly obscured by plants. This trail passes an aquatic-bird habitat, a series of shallow ponds and marshes. At its end, the trail connects with a steep switchback path that bends uphill and back into the main park.

If you'd like an easier trod to and from the beach, follow this part of the walk in reverse, as follows: where Discovery Park Blvd. bends northwest, turn onto a side path that starts parallel on

Side Trip: Shilshole and Golden Gardens

For more Puget Sound scenery, keep walking west on the Burke-Gilman Trail beyond this walk's official end point at 32nd Ave. NW. The trail bends north along the shore. Within 0.5 mile you're at the waterfront restaurant Ray's Boathouse, the start of the Shilshole strip. Another 0.5 mile and you're at the Shilshole Bay Marina, packed with docked pleasure boats and watched over by a statue of legendary explorer Leif Erikson. The trail ends another 0.75 mile north, at Golden Gardens Park. This long stretch of beach and forested hillside trails is popular year-round.

the road's right side. This path bends north to the steep path down the bluff to the beach. Turn southwest along the shoreline to the lighthouse. Turn east onto Discovery Park Blvd., winding gently uphill back to the beginning of the side path. Take a hard left, heading northbound this time, and in less than 0.5 mile, you'll see Daybreak Star, as noted below, to your left.

Coming from North Beach, at the top of the hill, the trail leading from the hill climb forks. Take the left (south-southeastern) fork to another paved road. Beyond that, you find a concrete restroom structure to your left. Beyond that, turn left onto the Loop Trail. Take another left onto another paved road heading north.

This road takes you toward the southern side of the ❸ Daybreak Star Indian Cultural Center. The United Indians of All Tribes Foundation established the arts and educational facility in 1973 after American Indian activists staged a 1970 sit-in on the soon-to-be-abandoned fort property. Take a left onto the center's grounds, around the striking angular building (resembling an eight-sided star) with tribal motifs within and without.

Turn right on the road north of Daybreak Star, heading east then bending southeast. You're soon surrounded by another thickly forested area. See if you can spot some of the many small and large birds in the park (more than 200 different species, according to the Seattle Audubon Society). This unnamed road intersects with Texas Way. If you want to end your walk now, take a right onto Texas Way to a route 33 bus stop. Or you can turn south from that bus stop and onto Illinois Ave., which leads back to Washington Ave. and the park's east entrance.

To continue with this walk's second leg, turn east (left) on Texas Way, then north (left) on 10th Ave. W. and out of the park. Turn east (right) onto W. Commodore Way. On its north side are some large waterfront homes, many equipped with their own private boat docks. Soon you pass under the lovely rust-colored iron lattice that is the BNSF Railway's Salmon Bay Bridge. The 1914 draw-bridge has a huge overhead counterweight on the north half of its single-truss superstructure.

This bridge's southern approach lies at the western end of Commodore Park, part of the ❹ **Ballard Locks'** spiffy grounds. Take the paved walk past the bushes and flower beds, east to the locks, and take a left.

Within the lower level of the locks' pedestrian passage, a dark room with big picture windows looks in on the fish ladder, built into the locks to help salmon return to spawn. You can view the ladder from above when you walk up the short outdoor ramp to the roof. A sculpture here by Paul Sorey called *Salmon Waves* depicts metallic ocean waves swirling up.

Spillway at the Ballard Locks

The fish ladder's roof is the entry to the locks' pedestrian passage. It takes you over the spillway structure, then, with swinging metal footbridges, across the two locks. Watch the boats enter the locks, whose water level is either filled or lowered. (The Corps of Engineers, which maintains the Lake Washington Ship Canal system, keeps the freshwater east of the locks 20 to 22 feet higher than the saltwater west of the locks.)

On the north side of the locks, depending on which footbridges are open, you could be east or west of a concrete castle. It's the locks' office and visitor center, and it happens to look like the Corps of Engineers' fortress logo. Take the sidewalk to its west, heading north through the Carl S. English Jr. Botanical Garden. The English-style garden holds more than 500 plant species from across the world.

Take this paved walk north and out of the locks' grounds, to NW 54th St. To your right is the ❺ **Lockspot Cafe,** a quaint seafood grill and bar. One block to your left, at 32nd Ave. NW, is ❻ **Red Mill Totem House,** a veteran fish-and-chips shop designed to imitate a Northwest tribal longhouse. The local Red Mill hamburger chain took over the space, serving Totem House's seafood specialties as well as Red Mill's burgers.

One block north, at 32nd and NW Market St., is a stop for bus route 17 to downtown.

This walk connects easily to two other walks. It starts 1.3 miles north of Walk 17 and ends 0.5 mile west of Walk 22.

Points of Interest

1 **Discovery Park Visitor Center** 3801 Discovery Park Blvd., 206-386-4236, seattle.gov/parks/find
/centers/discovery-park-environmental-learning-center

2 **West Point Lighthouse** At the foot of Utah Ave. in Discovery Park, 206-386-4236

3 **Daybreak Star Indian Cultural Center** 5011 Bernie Whitebear Way, 206-285-4425,
unitedindians.org

4 **Ballard (Hiram M. Chittenden) Locks** 3015 NW 54th St., 206-780-2500, nws.usace.army.mil

5 **Lockspot Cafe** 3005 NW 54th St., 206-789-4865, thelockspotcafe.com

6 **Red Mill Totem House** 3058 NW 54th St., 206-784-1400, redmillburgers.com

17 Magnolia
No "Bluffing"

BOUNDARIES: 27th Ave. W., W. Smith St., Perkins Lane W., and Magnolia Blvd. W.
DISTANCE: 3.25 miles
DIFFICULTY: Moderate (1 upward stairway)
PARKING: Free street parking
PUBLIC TRANSIT: Metro route 24 stops at 28th Ave. W. and W. McGraw St.

As the legend goes, while charting Puget Sound and its lands from his ship, British explorer George Vancouver spied some lovely magnolia trees rising atop a tall bluff on a peninsula at Elliott Bay's northern lip. Capt. Vancouver labeled that peninsula Magnolia. The name stuck, even though explorations on land confirmed that those were really madrona trees. Yet the name *Magnolia,* with its intimations of Southern gentility, fit what became a patrician village within the city, a home to spectacular views (and equally spectacular homes, many sporting a more mid-century modern sense of style than those on neighboring Queen Anne Hill). Another Seattle neighborhood was eventually named Madrona (Walk 28).

Walk Description

Start at ❶ **Ella Bailey Park,** 27th Ave. W. and W. Smith St. This recent addition to Seattle's park system reuses the playground of a now-closed school and offers a great view of Elliott Bay and the downtown skyline.

Turn west on Smith and go one block. Turn left (south) on 28th Ave. W. Pass the handsome brick front of the shuttered Magnolia Elementary and the intersection with the eastbound W. McGraw St., and reach the intersection with the westbound (and noncontiguous) W. McGraw St.

Walk west on McGraw, which at first is a solid middle class residential street heading downhill toward 31st Ave. W. There you find ❷ **Magnolia Lutheran Church**'s tall-pyramid spire and a more unassuming Latter-Day Saints church across from it.

One block west, at 32nd Ave. W., you reach Magnolia Village, the neighborhood's shopping district. The sidewalks here are lined with real, albeit nonnative, magnolia trees. Book readers (a population I presume you are among) will enjoy the homey ❸ **Magnolia's Bookstore.** This is also your only opportunity along this walk to fill (or empty) your body. Among your choices are the ❹ **Magnolia Village Pub,** the Yune sushi restaurant, Mexican café El Ranchon, and cozy Chinese restaurant ❺ **Gim Wah.**

Turn left (south) on 35th Ave. W. and go one block, toward the subdued ❻ **Episcopal Church of the Ascension.** Turn right (southwest) on Viewmont Way W. As the streets here become curvier, the houses become fancier.

At the intersection with Constance Dr. W., keep right. Viewmont Way W. here becomes West Viewmont Way W., winding northwest. (Seattle's street nomenclature, if you haven't already figured out, can have its quirks.) This street and those surrounding it are exceptionally wide, adding to the feeling of big-sky spaciousness.

Turn left (southwest) on W. Parkmont Pl., go two blocks, and turn right (northwest) onto Magnolia Blvd. W. To your right are big houses and small mansions in a wide variety of styles, from brick Tudor manors to suburban ranch houses on steroids. To your left, a long, grassy, public view corridor looks out toward the Olympic Peninsula and mountains, with benches and running paths and occasional make-out parking spots.

At the fork with W. Raye St., turn left. Raye winds downhill through the Magnolia Bluff greenbelt. You've gone instantly from a controlled world of urban luxury into the illusion of being in a deep, wild forest, among tall trees and wild vines. (A word of caution: This stretch of Raye is a narrow two-lane road without sidewalks.)

Raye ends at an intersection with Perkins Lane W. Turn southeast (left) on this curvy, one-lane road. Here the illusion of woodsy solitude is broken only by brief glimpses of the bay and by the driveways of residences, where urban hermits live in greater or lesser fear of mudslides. This fate occurred to several unlucky houses in the winter of 1996–97. That part of Perkins has remained closed. Just before the concrete barriers marking the end of the road, climb a long set of concrete steps heading up the hillside back to Magnolia Blvd.

Turn right to walk southeast on the west side of Magnolia Blvd., alongside the other walkers, runners, and cyclists enjoying the street's park side. (The only people you're likely to see outside on the other side, the side with the big houses and the well-manicured shrubbery, are gardeners and couriers.) Peering over the bluff, you may see the remnants of a Perkins Lane house that fell victim to a mudslide. Magnolia Blvd. then bends north toward W. Howe St.

Turn east on Howe, which becomes a short bridge over Pleasant Valley, a ravine between the peninsula's two hills. At the east end of this bridge is an intersection with a street that's labeled both Clise Pl. W. (northbound) and Magnolia Blvd. (southbound). The southwest corner of this intersection bears an entrance to ❼ **Magnolia Park,** a narrow, wooded park with an easy trail down to the bay.

From here you have three options: continue east on Howe four blocks to 28th (seven blocks south of this walk's start), continue on Howe three blocks to a 29 or 31 bus at 29th Ave. W., or take Clise north 0.25 mile back to Magnolia Village.

This walk connects easily to two other walks. At 35th Ave. W. and W. McGraw St., you are 1.3 miles south of Walk 16. From this walk's end, you can turn south on Magnolia Blvd. W., which bends east and leads to the Magnolia Bridge, down to Walk 3 (1.2 miles away).

Points of Interest

① **Ella Bailey Park** 27th Ave. W. and W. Smith St., seattle.gov/parks/find/parks/ella-bailey-park

② **Magnolia Lutheran Church** 2414 31st Ave. W., 206-284-0155, magnolialutheranchurch.com

③ **Magnolia's Bookstore** 3206 W. McGraw St., 206-283-1062, magnoliasbookstore.com

④ **Magnolia Village Pub** 3221 W. McGraw St., 206-285-9756, magnolia-villagepub.com

⑤ **Gim Wah** 3418 W. McGraw St., 206-284-7000

⑥ **Episcopal Church of the Ascension** 2330 Viewmont Way W., 206-283-3967, ascensionseattle.org

⑦ **Magnolia Park** 1461 Magnolia Blvd. W., seattle.gov/parks/find/parks/magnolia-park

18 Queen Anne Hill
Crowning Glory

Above: The famous view of downtown from Kerry Park

BOUNDARIES: 8th Ave. W., W. Raye St., Bigelow Ave. N., and Republican St.
DISTANCE: 4.5 miles
DIFFICULTY: Moderate (1 brief uphill segment)
PARKING: Free street parking
PUBLIC TRANSIT: Metro route 2 stops at 7th Ave. W. and W. Raye St.

Rising some 450 feet, Queen Anne is the tallest of Seattle's original seven hills. Its name comes from the ornate Victorian homes on its south slope, built to take advantage of some truly spectacular views. Atop the hill's view-deprived mesa, the housing stock tended to be more modest but still solid and respectable. This venerable middle-class neighborhood was becoming more regal even before the 2000s housing inflation. Today, you'll see an enticing mix of classic 20th-century homes, schools, and commercial architecture as you walk down lovely tree-lined streets and catch stunning views of the city and Puget Sound.

Walk Description

Start at 8th Ave. W. and W. Halladay St., outside the **❶ Seattle Church of Christ**. The exquisite 1926 octagon combines Spanish colonial and Byzantine influences. It's the first of several former Christian Science buildings on these walks. Walk north on 8th one block.

Turn right (east) on W. Raye St. past **❷ Mount Pleasant Cemetery**. Among those interred here are Seattle cofounders William and Sarah Bell, Children's Hospital cofounder Anna Herr Clise, and some of the ashes of labor organizer Joe Hill. It also has Jewish, Muslim, and Chinese burial areas.

Turn right (south) on 6th Ave. W. The vast majority of Seattle's 84 square miles are zoned as single-family neighborhoods. This typical street has low-rise houses, often Craftsman bungalows or similar styles, with well-groomed front yards and setback side lawns between each home. South of W. Smith St., Coe Elementary School is a 2003 structure resembling one that burned two years before. At W. McGraw St., Ken's Market could be described as either a huge deli-mart or tiny supermarket. At W. Crockett St., the stone-clad **❸ Targy's** is an unapologetic working-stiffs' tavern.

Turn left (east) on Crockett to 4th Ave. W., another pleasant street with trees and shrubbery. Turn left to go north one block. Turn right (east) on W. McGraw St., past the start of the Queen Anne business strip (which we'll cut back to).

At 1st Ave. N. (which, in Seattle's idiosyncratic street nomenclature, is two blocks east of 1st Ave. W.), take a left-right dogleg back onto McGraw. Beyond 2nd Ave. N., McGraw becomes a short bridge over a deep wooded ravine. Continue to the street-end viewpoint east of Bigelow Ave. N., featuring a stunning vista of Lake Union and Capitol Hill.

Backtrack to Bigelow and turn left (south). This is part of the Crown of Queen Anne, a scenic loop encircling the hill. At Boston St., notice the sweeping brick solidity of the Old Hay School. (The school district built a new Hay Elementary a few blocks away, then kept the old Hay as an alternative secondary school.) You might glimpse the Space Needle to the south.

Turn right on Boston. West of 3rd Ave. N., five attached skinny houses typify local townhome projects of the 2000s. A different townhome group at Warren Ave. N. makes four small homes look like one big one. Kitty-corner from there, a retirement home occupies the original 1908 and 1928 brick buildings of Seattle Children's Hospital (now in the Laurelhurst neighborhood).

Turn left on Queen Anne Ave. N. The neighborhood's main drag is also called the Counterbalance, after the gravity-assisted cable car that used to connect it with downtown. The street has gathered fashionable shops and restaurants but also remains a place for basic provisions.

East of Queen Anne Ave. at Galer St. is a pedestrian staircase. Take a left and climb it to 1st Ave. W. and Galer, and continue east. To your left, you see the new John Hay Elementary School.

To your right, the KOMO-TV transmitting tower stands just before the former Queen Anne High School (now condos). The 1909 neoclassical building typifies Progressive-era desires to edify as well as educate.

Turn right (south) on 2nd Ave. N., a narrow street with thick trees. It bends west into Highland Dr. At Highland and 1st Ave. N., the 1906 Polson mansion combines Arts and Crafts architecture with a turreted round tower on its view side. Across 1st Ave. N. is the Chappell House, built in a French Gothic motif.

As the views get better, the houses get ritzier. At the southwest corner of Queen Anne and Highland is the 1905 Harry W. Treat House. The 17,000-square-foot brick-and-stucco mansion is now divided into 15 apartments. Across the street, the white colonial Ballard mansion is also now apartments. The buildings built *as* apartments get fancier too, particularly the 1921 Victoria Apartments (now condos), a block-long, four-story brick estate with a meticulous front garden.

The next block up is ❹ **Kerry Park,** whose downtown-skyline vista is familiar to every *Frasier* viewer. Continue west on Highland, enjoying the variety of street trees and the stately Victorian and Queen Anne homes. ❺ **The Betty Bowen Viewpoint,** named for a local arts patron, lies at 7th Ave. W. Besides a stunning view toward Elliott Bay and the Pier 86 grain terminals (Walk 3), it has sidewalk mosaics representing Pacific Northwest artists.

Turn left (south) on 7th, a narrow cobblestone road. Take a left dogleg turn onto W. Prospect St., then promptly go right (southeast) on W. Kinnear Pl. To your left at 700 W. Kinnear, what was a large, tasteful 1900 home was recently enlarged and altered into an ostentatious monument to excess. You can see what it used to look like on an episode of HBO's *Six Feet Under.*

Turn southwest back onto 7th (another steep downhill brick road) to W. Olympic Pl. At the northeast corner are the Chelsea Apartments, a 1907 English Renaissance hotel building. Across Olympic lies Kinnear Park, with another lookout toward Elliott Bay (restrooms are in a dugout structure beneath the lookout).

Turn left (southeast) on Olympic, which soon bends east. At Olympic and 5th Ave. W., a new row of faux-Tudor townhomes tries to fit in alongside older, Spanish mission–style apartments. At 2nd Ave. W., the 1909 De la Mar Apartments are four stories of neoclassical stateliness with marble floors and stained glass windows. You are forgiven if you mistake the building for a European embassy.

Turn right (south) on 2nd, and continue past several modest prewar apartment low-rises. Turn left (east) onto W. Roy St., to an old brick church that's now ❻ **On the Boards,** home to contemporary dance and performance art. The Sitting Room, an intimate bistro-bar, is on its ground floor.

Turn right (south) on 1st Ave. W. and go one block to W. Mercer St. and ❼ **Ozzie's Diner,** a burger and pizza joint and karaoke bar. On its north wall a bizarre mural shows a quaint old-timey family, drinking peacefully out of doors.

Turn east on Mercer to Queen Anne Ave., the heart of the Lower Queen Anne business district (also known as Uptown). At the northeast corner of Queen Anne and Mercer, the MarQueen Hotel occupies a block-long brick former apartment building. Near the northwest corner, **❽ Peso's** Mexican restaurant sports iconic wrought-iron art.

Turn right (south) on Queen Anne Ave. N. On this block are the Mecca Cafe (down-home cooking and strong drinks), the Uptown Espresso chain's flagship branch, the SIFF Cinema Uptown, and the only **❾ Dick's Drive-In** (Walks 10 and 21) to offer indoor seating. At Republican St., turn left (east) and walk one block to 1st Ave. N., where two 1929 apartment buildings are now the Inn at Queen Anne.

Go left (north) onto 1st. To your left are some popular restaurants, including Racha Noodles (Thai) and T. S. McHugh's (upmarket pub grub). At 1st and Mercer is a Metropolitan Market strip mall.

Turn left (west) on Roy. To your left is the modern arced A-frame of **❿ St. Paul's Episcopal Church**. The parish has been around since 1892; this building was built in 1962 to coincide with the world's fair. It sports a public garden with a circular concrete labyrinth.

Continue on Roy to Queen Anne Ave. and Counterbalance Park, named in honor of the old cable-car line. In the 1980s, it was the site of a Dr. Seuss–esque restaurant building, which disapproving residents unofficially called the blob.

To return to your start, backtrack to the northeast corner of 1st and Mercer and take a 2 bus to 7th and Raye.

This walk connects easily to two other walks. It ends near Walk 7. At Queen Anne Ave. and Republican you're four blocks north and three blocks northwest of Walk 3.

Points of Interest

1 **Seattle Church of Christ** 2555 8th Ave. W., 206-914-2660, seattlechurchofchrist.org

2 **Mount Pleasant Cemetery** 700 W. Raye St., 206-282-1270

3 **Targy's** 600 W. Crockett St., 206-352-8882, targys.com

4 **Kerry Park** 211 W. Highland Dr., seattle.gov/parks/find/parks/kerry-park

5 **Betty Bowen Viewpoint** 1191 7th Ave. W., 206-684-4075, seattle.gov/parks/find/parks/marshall-park

6 **On the Boards** 100 W. Roy St., 206-217-9886, ontheboards.org

7 **Ozzie's Diner** 105 W. Mercer St., 206-284-4618, ozziesinseattle.com

8 **Peso's** 605 Queen Anne Ave. N., 206-283-9353, pesoskitchenandlounge.com

9 **Dick's Drive-In** 500 Queen Anne Ave. N., 206-285-5155, dicksdrivein.com

10 **St. Paul's Episcopal Church** 15 Roy St., 206-282-0786, stpaulseattle.org

19 Fremont
Still Funky but Chic

BOUNDARIES: N. 43rd St., N. Canal St., N. Northlake Way, and Wallingford Ave. N.
DISTANCE: 3.75 miles
DIFFICULTY: Moderate (brief inclines at the beginning and end)
PARKING: Metered street parking
PUBLIC TRANSIT: Metro routes 31, 32, 40, and 62 stop at Fremont Ave. N. and N. 34th St.

A once-separate mill town annexed to Seattle, Fremont fell into a long decline after 1932, when the Aurora Bridge diverted traffic away from the neighborhood. It became a hangout for fringe populations. Those subcultures eventually included collegiate hippies, who brought funky shops and arts studios to the neighborhood. More recently, it's become a nightlife and dining destination, promoting itself as the Center of the Universe. Its most famous attraction is the annual Solstice Parade, with artsy floats, alternative marching bands, and body-painted cyclists. Even during the rest of the year, Fremont prides itself on doing things with a little more eccentricity and a little more flair, as you're about to see.

Walk Description

Start under the ❶ **Fremont Rocket** at N. 35th St. and Evanston Ave. N. This 55-foot-tall space-age decorative sign used to adorn a now-demolished surplus store in Belltown (Walk 7). It stands atop one of Fremont's several art and fashion boutiques, **Burnt Sugar**. Turn south one block on Evanston, past the T-shirt store Destee Nation.

Turn left (east) onto the north side of N. 34th St. Behind you is the Red Door Alehouse, highlighted by a replica of the red R sign that once stood atop the Rainier brewery in SoDo. To your left at Fremont Ave. N. is the neighborhood's main shopping drag (which we'll track back to). To your right is the Fremont Bridge. The neighborhood's chief icon was built (along with the Lake Washington Ship Canal it crosses) in 1917. It's one of the busiest drawbridges in the United States, rising an average of 35 times a day.

Cross Fremont Ave., then cross 34th. At a traffic island in this crossing you meet *Waiting for the Interurban*, Richard Beyer's 1979 aluminum sculpture commemorating the long-gone streetcar line that ran up Fremont Ave. It depicts five people and a dog standing beneath a shelter; the dog's face resembles community organizer Arman Stepanian. You might see decor and fashion accessories added to the figures by citizens to denote special occasions.

Cross to the south side of 34th and resume walking east, past one of the office parks that replaced the lumber mills. Halfway down this long block you find a latter-day sequel sculpture, *Late for the Interurban*. It depicts J. P. Patches and Gertrude, clown stars of a legendary local kids' TV show that ran from 1958 to 1981.

Turn back from there and then turn right (north) onto Fremont Ave., past quaint old shop buildings (and modern mixed-use buildings trying to fit in), housing Thai, teriyaki, and sushi restaurants and merchants selling hammered dulcimers, fashion jewelry, and vinyl records.

At N. 36th St. (with the Hotel Hotel hostel and its downstairs Fremont Tavern), turn right (east) and uphill, past the Fremont Baptist Church's blocky brick solidity, to the *Fremont Troll*. The 1990 concrete sculpture, commissioned from four local artists, was built to turn the vacant land under the Aurora Bridge from blight to tourist attraction. The whole thing's 16 feet tall; the troll's one eye is a hubcap; the car in its paw is a real VW Beetle.

Turn right (south) on Troll Ave. to N. 35th St.; turn right (west) onto the south side of 35th, passing an elegant Spanish mission–style ❷ **Seattle Public Library** branch. Beyond it is a new pocket park with a circular walkway. Beyond that is the intimate Agrodolce Sicilian bistro. Beyond that, enjoy artist Parris Broderick's cartoony 1991 mural advertising the bistro's defunct predecessor, Still Life in Fremont.

You're now at the five-way intersection of 35th, Fremont Ave., and Fremont Pl. N. Cross to the west side of Fremont Ave. to the Portage Bay Goods card and gift store. Take a right across 35th to the north side of Fremont Pl. Turn left (northwest), past a triangular building containing an eyeglasses store and Espresso To Go (the most ornate tiny coffee stand you'll see anywhere).

Across an alley stands a 16-foot bronze sculpture of Vladimir Lenin. A local collector acquired this monument of strident kitsch from a Slovakian scrapyard in 1993, literally rescuing it from the trash heap of history.

Fremont Pl. bends west-northwest and becomes N. 36th St. To your right, the sedate grounds of a funeral home belie the noisy place this street can be after sundown. To your left, the reclaimed neon sign of a 1950s bathing beauty marks ❸ **High Dive,** the first of the street's live-music clubs.

Continue on 36th beyond Dayton Ave. N. On your right, a former supermarket holds Roxy's Diner (originally a deli specializing in New York–style sandwiches, now grown to a full-service restaurant with a speakeasy-esque bar in the back). West of this are Ballroom (a swank bar and pool hall) and a Caffe Ladro. On the left side, ❹ **Fremont Coffee Company** occupies an entire historic bungalow.

On the north side of 36th beyond Francis Ave. N., ❺ **Nectar** is a music club with a covered outdoor patio. West of Phinney Ave. N., the ❻ **George and Dragon** anchors several pubs that cater to hard-core soccer fans. All are regularly packed during Sounders FC matches.

Two blocks beyond the George and Dragon, 36th bends northwest again and becomes Leary Way NW. Continue as Leary segues from light-industrial to residential. Let your inner 8-year-old snicker at the sign for Tacoma Screw Products, then let your inner 4-year-old be awed by the life-size bear statues in front of the Brown Bear Car Wash.

At 4320 Leary, an unmarked triangular 1920s building houses a recording studio that's had many names and owners since 1978. The first Nirvana and Soundgarden albums, among hundreds of others, were made there. Death Cab for Cutie guitarist Chris Walla now runs it.

Take a left onto NW 43rd St., along the south side of the ❼ **Hale's Ales Brewery and Pub.** Its back warehouse is seasonally used as a performance space. At its circus-decor entrance take a left onto the Burke-Gilman Trail, a former rail right-of-way that's become a popular walking, jogging, and biking path. Your first blocks along the Burke-Gilman abut warehouses, rail sidings, and a cement plant. Shrubbery and small trees have been added along the trail's sides to make it look at least a little green.

Once the trail parallels the north side of the Ship Canal, you're among wide lawns with a variety of trees, hugging the water, and can spot ducks, kayaks, and yachts. At Phinney Ave. N., the park sports two wire-frame dinosaurs (built for a Pacific Science Center exhibit), increasingly covered in topiary ivy. Here you can also take a one-block detour left on Phinney to Theo Chocolates or Brouwer's Cafe (a Belgian-style pub).

Continue or resume along the Burke-Gilman. To your left are the office-park buildings built where Fremont's sawmills had been. The trail bends under the ❽ **Fremont Bridge,** then curves north into park space under the Aurora Bridge's pillars. It then bends inland (right) from the Ship Canal.

At Stone Way N. (now the site of several modern cafés and bars), take a short right-left dogleg closer to the water, along the walking and biking lane of N. Northlake Way. You see some marinas and the former Lake Deli Mart building (a classic corrugated-steel Quonset hut).

Continue on Northlake to ❾ **Gas Works Park.** This green jewel on Lake Union's northern crown was reclaimed in the 1970s from a coal gasification plant, rendered surplus when natural-gas pipelines reached the Pacific Northwest. A few pieces of the plant have been preserved as industrial sculpture within the park, which is otherwise given to open spaces and picnic tables.

From here you can backtrack to the Stone Way bar strip or the Fremont retail core. Alternately, climb an outdoor staircase connecting Northlake with Wallingford Ave. N. From the top of the steps, walk uphill on Wallingford. At the northwest corner of Wallingford and N. 35th St. is a 31/32 bus stop, leading back to Fremont Ave.

This walk connects easily to four other walks. At N. 36th and Fremont you're 0.5 mile south of Walk 20. At 36th and Troll you're 0.5 mile south-southeast of Walk 21. At the Burke-Gilman Trail and 43rd you're 0.5 mile southeast of Walk 22. At Northlake and Wallingford you're 0.75 mile west of Walk 25.

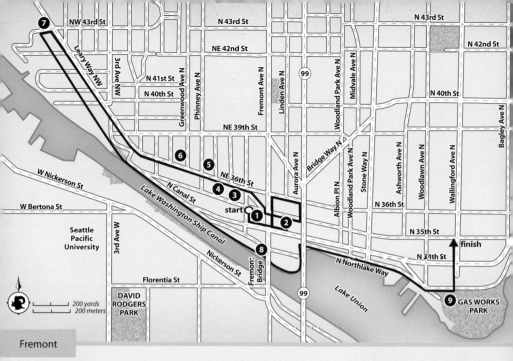

Points of Interest

1 Fremont Rocket and Burnt Sugar 601 N. 35th St., 206-545-0699, burntsugar.us

2 Seattle Public Library, Fremont Branch 731 N. 35th St., spl.org

3 High Dive 513 N. 36th St., 206-632-0212, highdiveseattle.com

4 Fremont Coffee Company 459 N. 36th St., 206-632-3633, fremontcoffee.net

5 Nectar 412 N. 36th St., 206-632-2020, nectarlounge.com

6 George & Dragon Pub 206 N. 36th St, 206-545-6864, georgeanddragonpub.com

7 Hale's Ales Brewery & Pub 4301 Leary Way NW, 206-782-0737, halesbrewery.com

8 Fremont Bridge Fremont Ave. N., south of N. Northlake Way, seattle.gov/transportation/bridges.htm

9 Gas Works Park 2101 N. Northlake Way, seattle.gov/parks/find/parks/gas-works-park

20 Phinney Ridge and Greenwood
It's a Zoo Out Here

BOUNDARIES: N. 42nd St., Fremont Ave. N., 1st Ave. NW, and N. 87th St.
DISTANCE: 3 miles
DIFFICULTY: Moderate (1 short incline at the start)
PARKING: Free street parking along Fremont Ave. N. and surrounding streets; $5 parking in
   Woodland Park south lot
PUBLIC TRANSIT: Metro route 5 stops at this walk's start.

Phinney Ridge is North Seattle's topographic "spine," rising 2 miles between the traditionally industrial Ballard and Fremont and the traditionally more bourgeois northeast neighborhoods. At the ridge's peak stands the Woodland Park Zoo, a crossroads of species as well as cultures. It's a worldwide leader in showcasing its various critters within naturalistic habitat displays. Before and after passing the zoo, this walk takes you through some neighborhood business blocks that have gradually become more boutique-y in recent years.

Walk Description

Start at N. 42nd St. and Fremont Ave. N., near the former Roux bistro's frontier-style 1908 wood building (previously the Buckaroo Tavern) and the ❶ **Paseo Caribbean Food** (a walk-up Cuban sandwich shop with major lines at lunchtime). It's the start of a cozy little business district, which includes some fine dining spots, a major musical instrument store, and a jam-packed deli-mart. Its newest *and* oldest attraction is the ❷ **Fremont Abbey Arts Center**, a performance and workshop space in a 1914 brick church building.

Walk north on Fremont to N. 50th St., the south border of Woodland Park. The 92-acre park was originally the private estate of developer Guy Phinney. The city bought the land from his widow, then developed it according to the Olmsted Brothers' citywide park plan, with the ❸ **Woodland Park Zoo** as its centerpiece. The zoo's side entrance is here. So are a few free parking spaces outside the zoo's gates. Of particular note is the exquisitely landscaped rose garden east of the zoo entrance, with two white fountains and an Art Deco relief mural.

Turn left (west) along the park's south side, past an oversize bronze statue of a Spanish-American War soldier, to Phinney Ave. N. Turn right (north) along Phinney's east side, past the zoo's main entrance. Woodland Park is one of the nation's most renowned zoological parks, a leader in immersion exhibits that simulate animals' natural habitats. It's also a great walking site in its own right. But for this walk continue along Phinney. Woodland Park's northwest corner, at Phinney and N. 59th St., is another public open space outside the zoo's fences.

Continue north along Phinney, into a neighborhood business strip flourishing with gift boutiques, small apparel shops, and cool eating and drinking spots. The latter category's grande dame is Sully's Snowgoose Saloon (formerly La Boheme), at Phinney and N. 62nd St. The post-Prohibition-era tavern looks like a Tudor cottage on the outside and a ski lodge on the inside. Another favorite is Teasome, offering seafood and Asian fusion dishes near N. 65th St. A block north of that is the ❹ **Phinney Neighborhood Center,** an arts and community meeting space in a preserved wooden schoolhouse.

At N. 67th St., follow the arterial as it doglegs into Greenwood Ave. N. Along the north end of this curving transitional segment is Red Mill Burgers, whose hearty handmade fare attracts long lines on weekend afternoons. Just beyond the S-curve on Greenwood's west side, a former art-gallery storefront now sells healing essentials.

Continue north on Greenwood, a pleasant stroll alongside more shops and eateries. The latter range from El Chupacabra's creative Mexican fare to the Goat on Greenwood's Southern comfort food. The former include stores selling clothes by local designers, shoes, pianos, antiques, rugs, knitting supplies, toys, pet supplies, greeting cards, picture frames, and baked goods. Then there's a business best described as "only in Seattle"—Espresso Dental, where you can get wide awake before you get numbed.

At Greenwood and N. 79th St. turn left (west) and continue for one long block, to 1st Ave. NW and the stately Romanesque edifice of ❺ **St. John the Evangelist Catholic Church** with its dome-topped square tower. Turn right (north) on 1st to N. 83rd St. and a very different take on religious architecture at the ❻ **Sakya Monastery of Tibetan Buddhism**. It's a 1920s Presbyterian church building that's been completely redone and repainted in the traditional bright Tibetan colors. A large bell-shaped stupa (a sacred container with other sacred objects placed inside it) sits at its front. It's one of many holy objects from India, Tibet, and Nepal adorning the building inside and out.

Continuing north on 1st, you soon view the huge red sign for the Fred Meyer big-box store on N. 85th St., anchor of the main Greenwood business district. Turn right (east) on 85th, through an old-fashioned main street district. On the north side, a onetime neighborhood cinema now houses Taproot Theater, a mainstream Christian troupe staging drawing-room comedies and moral-choice dramas.

Cross to the southeast corner of 85th and Greenwood. Just south of this corner (and north of the Angry Beaver hockey bar), a busy, bizarre storefront proclaims itself to be Greenwood Space Travel Supply Co. and promises rocket parking on the roof. It's really a kids' writing and educational center. Formerly part of author-publisher Dave Eggers's 826 group, it's now the independent ❼ **Bureau of Fearless Ideas (BFI)**. The fake sci-fi advertising is intended to enthrall kids with the power of words even before they step inside.

Turn back north on Greenwood, north of 85th. You're now outside Seattle's pre-1954 city limits, and in a one-block nightlife minimecca. Your dinner-and-drink choices range from the unapologetically working-class (❽ **Baranof,** with retro nautical-themed murals and decorations in both its diner and barrooms) to spiffy (Gainsbourg, the Olive and Grape) to handcrafted (Naked City Brewery & Alehouse). There's shopping too—used books, games, hobbies, and Mexican groceries.

At the northwest corner of Greenwood and N. 87th St., you can take a 5 bus back to your starting point.

This walk connects easily to three other walks. It starts 0.5 mile north of Walk 19. At N. 46th St. and Fremont you're 0.5 mile west of Walk 21. At N. 77th St. and Greenwood Ave. N. you're a downhill 0.5 mile west of Walk 23.

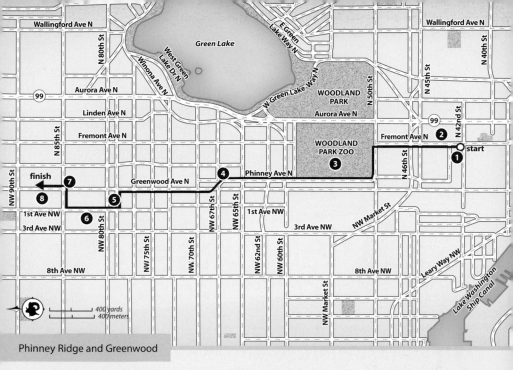

Phinney Ridge and Greenwood

Points of Interest

1. **Paseo** 4225 Fremont Ave. N., 206-545-7440, paseorestaurants.com
2. **Fremont Abbey Arts Center** 4272 Fremont Ave. N., 206-414-8325, fremontabbey.org
3. **Woodland Park Zoo** 5500 Phinney Ave. N., 206-548-2500, zoo.org
4. **Phinney Neighborhood Center** 6532 Phinney Ave. N., 206-783-2244, phinneycenter.org
5. **St. John the Evangelist Catholic Church** 121 N. 80th St., 206-782 2810, stjohnsea.org
6. **Sakya Monastery of Tibetan Buddhism** 108 NW 83rd St., 206-789-2573, sakya.org
7. **Bureau of Fearless Ideas** 8414 Greenwood Ave. N., 206-725-2625, fearlessideas.org
8. **Baranof** 8549 Greenwood Ave. N., 206-782-9260

21 Wallingford to Roosevelt
Rubber Chickens and Video Nostalgia

Above: *The original Dick's Drive-In*

BOUNDARIES: N. 44th St., Stone Way N., NE 53rd St., and Roosevelt Way NE
DISTANCE: 2.25 miles
DIFFICULTY: Easy (2 slight inclines)
PARKING: Limited free street parking
PUBLIC TRANSIT: Metro routes 44 and 62 stop near the walk's start at N. 45th St. and Stone Way N.

Unlike the founders of Ballard and Fremont, John Wallingford wasn't an industrialist. He was a real estate dealer. He and his fellow developers platted a streetcar suburb between Lake Union and Green Lake. It became a bedroom community with one of the strongest concentrations of Craftsman bungalows (early Seattle's favorite home style). Here, families drawn by Lake Union's industry mingled with the University of Washington community. Later, Wallingford became a stronghold of aging hippies; you're still more likely to spot a gray male ponytail here than any-where in town. It now hosts an ever-changing array of small shops and cafés. One of your last stops will be a video store where you can get DVDs filmed in one language, dubbed in another, and subtitled in a third (none of them English).

Walk Description

Start in front of Lincoln High School, at N. 44th St. and Interlake Ave. N. The Edwardian brick edifice was a regular high school from 1907 to 1981. By the late 1980s it was depicted as a gang-ridden wasteland in the horror film *Class of 1999*. The school district then used it as an interim replacement for schools whose own buildings are being remodeled, before turning it back into a regular high school.

Go west one block on 44th to Stone Way N. (the only Seattle street with the same name as Fred Flintstone's piano), by a big hardware store. Turn right (north) and continue two blocks on Stone to N. 45th St. Three corners of this intersection hold big recent mixed-use buildings. But you're headed to the oldest building here, a former state liquor store at the northeast corner. You won't miss its bright red-and-yellow paint job, or the friendly monsters painted on top of that. This is ❶ **Archie McPhee,** a gift, toy, and souvenir store unlike any other. Tofu mints! Nacho lip balm! Gummy bacon! Plastic pickles emitting yodeling noises! Dashboard Jesus dolls! Inflatable toast! A Crazy Cat Lady action figure! Stuffed latex vultures! You might want to linger for hours, but you have places to go.

Turn right and walk east along the north side of 45th. Beyond Interlake Ave. N. is the Alphabet Soup children's bookstore, one of several storefronts on this street inside classic Craftsman bungalows. Beyond Woodlawn Ave. N. stands Sun Cleaners' bright sunburst sign. Two buildings away, the May Thai restaurant was designed to look like an ornate suburban Thai home. At Densmore Ave. N., the 45th Street Community Clinic occupies a comely, two-story old fire station. Kitty-corner from there, a Spanish-style row of storefronts includes great beer and wine stores.

Continue on the north side of 45th past Wallingford Ave. N., where a two-story QFC supermarket bears some non-chain-standard signage: giant neon block letters spelling WALLINGFORD. In 2000 QFC was buying neighborhood stores around town, including this site's prior occupant, Food Giant. Neighborhood activists demanded the new owners keep the food giant sign, a local landmark since the 1950s. This compromise incorporates seven of the old sign's nine letters. Across at the southeast corner of 45th and Wallingford, a big wood elementary school was revamped in the 1980s into the Wallingford Center mall.

Beyond Burke Ave. N. are a rug gallery, two Japanese restaurants, a walk-up taco bar, and Murphy's, a neighborhood Irish bar. Beyond Meridian Ave. N. are the two Guild 45th Theater buildings (now closed). Between them is the Octopus Bar, in a 1913 bungalow. On the next block, the ❷ **Seamonster Lounge** serves up an eclectic live-music mix almost every night.

Turn left (north) on Bagley Ave. N., a narrow residential street. Just beyond N. 46th St., there's a dead end for drivers; keep walking into Meridian Park. It's the former grounds of a Catholic girls' home, the Home of the Good Shepherd (1906–1973). Here on the grounds' back side are a playground (with sculptures depicting children's-book characters), an apple orchard, gardens, and a P-Patch community garden. The home's manor house–style main building looms to your right. It's now the ❸ **Good Shepherd Center,** run by preservation group Historic Seattle. Its vast square footage includes a performance space (in the former chapel), artist and senior housing units, community-group offices, a yoga center, and a private K–5 school.

Take a right turn around the north side of the Good Shepherd Center, then another right toward the massive edifice's east entrance. Take a left down its front promenade, out of the grounds and onto Sunnyside Ave. N. Turn right (south) on Sunnyside. At N. 46th St. is the small, classy Elim Baptist Church. At 45th and Sunnyside, the Stop & Shop convenience store has one of Seattle's many recently opened *poke* cafés in the back.

Turn left to resume walking east on 45th. ❹ **Open Books,** an all-poetry bookstore, occupies the attached garage of an old house just beyond Sunnyside. Beyond 1st Ave. NE, the original ❺ **Dick's Drive-In** has supplied great cheap burgers and fries since 1954. Across from it on 2nd Ave. NE, ❻ **Golden Oldies Records** ("Open Eight Days a Week") is a trove of collectible vinyl; its wall bears regularly repainted rock-icon murals.

East of Thackeray Pl. NE, the Hawai'i General Store and Gallery offers both authentic and tourist-culture gifts and foods from the islands.

Continue on the north side of what's now NE 45th St., across the I-5 overpass. Just beyond 7th Ave. NE, the Seattle Go Center teaches the Japanese board game as a metaphor for life. Just east of there, turn your internal clock back to 1971 at the ❼ **Blue Moon Tavern,** Seattle's venerable literary-hippie dive bar. At 9th Ave. NE, an AMC Cinemas 10-plex anchors a retail complex on the former site of a Chevrolet dealership. The ex-Chevy showroom, at 45th and Roosevelt Way NE, now houses a bicycle shop.

Turn left (north) along the west side of Roosevelt Way. At NE 50th St., the Seven Gables Theater building (now closed, as is the Guild 45th) has only six gables. Across 50th, the Seattle Public Library's University Branch is an always-welcome instance of a stock Carnegie-funded library design. Cross to Roosevelt's east side and continue north to ❽ **Scarecrow Video**. Claiming more than 100,000 titles in stock (including many foreign films unreleased in this country), it's been called the best video store in the United States. With the home-video industry's nationwide decline, Scarecrow has become a nonprofit outfit dedicated to helping preserve the world's video/film heritage.

Walking on Roosevelt toward NE 53rd St., to your left is the **❾ Blessed Sacrament Catholic Church**'s imposing spire. To your right is a longtime comedy club, currently known as Laughs. To return to your start, backtrack south on Roosevelt to 45th and take a 44 bus to Stone Way.

This walk connects easily to four other walks in this book. It starts 0.5 mile north of Walk 19 and ends 0.25 mile south of Walk 24. At 50th and Roosevelt you're four blocks west of Walk 25. At the Good Shepherd Center you're 0.75 mile south of Walk 23.

The Italianate-style Good Shepherd Center, formerly a Catholic girls' home, is now a multipurpose community center comprising performance space, housing units, and a private school.

Points of Interest

1 **Archie McPhee** 1300 N. 45th St., 206-297-0240, archiemcpheeseattle.com

2 **Seamonster Lounge** 2202 N. 45th St., 206-992-1120, seamonsterlounge.com

3 **Good Shepherd Center** 4649 Sunnyside Ave. N., historicseattle.org/projects/gsc.aspx

4 **Open Books** 2414 N. 45th St., 206-633-0811, openpoetrybooks.com

5 **Dick's Drive-In** 111 NE 45th St., 206-634-0300, dicksdrivein.com

6 **Golden Oldies Records** 201 NE 45th St., 206-547-2260, goldenoldiesrecords.net

7 **Blue Moon Tavern** 712 NE 45th St., 206-675-9116, bluemoonseattle.wordpress.com

8 **Scarecrow Video** 5030 Roosevelt Way NE, 206-524-8554, scarecrow.com

9 **Blessed Sacrament Church** 5050 8th Ave. NE, 206-547-3020, blessed-sacrament.org

22 Ballard
The New and the Nordic

Above: *Mike's Chili Parlor Tavern, surrounded by newer retail-office development*

BOUNDARIES: NW 70th St., 24th Ave. NW, Ballard Ave. NW, NW 46th St., 14th Ave. NW
DISTANCE: 3.25 miles
DIFFICULTY: Easy (flat or downhill)
PARKING: Free street parking
PUBLIC TRANSIT: Metro routes 15 and RapidRide D stop at this walk's start.

A local bumper sticker in the mid-2000s read, "We in Ballard welcome our new condo overlords." Archie McPhee, a novelty store that later moved to Wallingford (Walk 21), sold the sticker. Archie's left a neighborhood that had originally developed around fishing, sawmills, and Scandinavian immigrant families. Having mostly survived the condo onslaught, it's now a quiet bedroom community, the spiritual home of the Seattle and Alaska fishing fleet, a quaint arts and shopping spot, and a happening nightlife zone. We start with the residential section (with some ethnic shopping and dining), then join a historic cobblestoned main street before ending up in the neighborhood's more modern main drag.

Walk Description

Start on the east side of 15th Ave. NW, south of 70th St., and walk south on 15th. ❶ **Scandinavian Specialties,** an unassuming storefront north of NW 67th St., is packed with Norse gifts and foods (packaged, takeout, or eat-in). The block after that belongs to Ballard High School, home to the fighting Ballard Beavers.

At 15th and NW 65th St., the onetime Zesto's Burger and Fish House is now the Mexican spot ❷ **El Camion.** At NW 58th St., ❸ **St. Alphonsus Parish'**s sleek, modern curves provide a fine contrast to the parish school behind it, an Edwardian brick schoolhouse.

Turn left on NW 52nd St. in front of another Amazon Fresh pick-up station. Look to the north side of 52nd for a mural of a dark-skinned earth goddess staring back at you. It draws you toward ❹ **Ballard Reuse,** vendors of used building materials, furnishings, and decor. East of that stands a bold neon sign exhorting you to ADD BARDAHL. It marks the headquarters of Bardahl Manufacturing, makers of motor-oil additives and related products since the 1930s. The building's clad in green plastic paneling, a mid-century style that hasn't come back into fashion.

Turn right (south) on 14th Ave. NW. At 14th and NW Leary Way, you can easily miss ❺ **Quest (formerly Mars Hill) Church,** a black warehouse building with minimal signage. Inside is a contemporary megachurch that markets the evangelical faith to the young and hip. At NW 46th St. you have an easier time finding the Salty Dog art and pottery studio; its front sports a mural of a theater curtain.

Turn right (west) on 46th to reach the Ballard Blocks retail project. Devised at the peak of the real estate boom, it's two hulking big-box structures. Walk west past its central corridor to view the Ballard "spite house," a small bungalow whose elderly owner refused to sell to the developers. (She died before the completion of Ballard Blocks, which was built around her property.)

Turn right (north) on 15th toward ❻ **Mike's Chili Parlor Tavern.** The same family has owned this working folks' pub with working folks' grub for more than nine decades. Its brick-and-neon storefront proves Deco-derived design can be manly. Continue on 15th one more block, then turn left (west) on NW Leary Way, under the Ballard Bridge's northern end. The 1917-built double drawbridge over the Lake Washington Ship Canal is a great 0.5-mile walk by itself. At its southern end is Fishermen's Terminal, home to the Seattle and Alaska fishing fleets.

If you're continuing with this walk, keep going west on Leary. Look on Leary's south side for another vintage neon sign, promoting Craig's Auto Springs. Near 17th Ave. NW, a neon horse head sticks out from the 1940s wooden shed now housing the Bergschrund brewpub.

Take a dogleg left (south) on 17th to NW 48th St., then turn right (west) on 48th to Ballard Ave. NW and hang a right, turning northwest into the Ballard Ave. historic district. Neglect, for the most part, preserved these six blocks of old bars, hardware stores, and residential hotels for decades. In recent years, it's become a site for nightlife and art.

In the first block you see some surviving machine shops and paint warehouses. Just beyond NW Dock St., Bad Albert's Tap & Grill marks the start of the bar-and-shopping strip. Across from it is Ethan Stowell's Ballard Pizza Co.

At the northeast corner of Ballard and NW Ione Pl., local celebrity chef Kathy Casey has her deli and wine shop. Next to that is the Conor Byrne Pub and its antique wooden back bar. Next to that is the Lock and Keel, a nautical-themed bar and BBQ joint with a 30-foot rowboat hanging from the ceiling. Next to that, Monster Art and Clothing stands behind an ornate 1893 facade.

Beyond 20th Ave. NW, King's Hardware starts a string of bars. They're anchored by the ❼ **Tractor Tavern,** a venerable live music club. Northwest from there, drinkers at Hattie's Hat and Percy's & Co. are often found peering across the street at a 1910 Elks building, where Olympic Health Club members toil behind big picture windows day and night.

Ballard Ave. then becomes a casual diner's dream, offering French cuisine, deluxe sandwiches, and sushi. There's funky shopping, too, including shoes, modern and retro furniture, fashion jewelry, garden accessories, handmade European toys, and musical instruments.

At the northeast corner of Ballard and 22nd Ave. NW is a pocket park called Marvin's Garden, a concrete patio with benches anchored by a short bell tower enclosing the half-ton brass bell from the old Ballard City Hall. It was named for Marvin Sjoberg, a colorful local character and self-proclaimed mayor of Ballard (decades after Seattle annexed the former independent town). The block continues with live music at the ❽ **Sunset Tavern,** drinks and German grub at the People's Pub, ethnic eats at La Carta de Oaxaca, and swank food and drink at Jones Brothers and Co. Ballard Ave. bends north just before it ends at NW Market St.

Turn left (west) on Market, passing the Pestle Rock Thai restaurant, to 24th Ave. NW. Turn left (south) and go one block to ❾ **Push/Pull,** a DIY gallery and art-creation space.

Head back north on the east side of 24th, past the used fashion and furniture store Classic Consignment and a particularly massive big-box condo.

Turn right onto the south side of NW 57th St., around the side of that big-box condo. Just east of it stands ❿ **Leif Erikson Lodge**. The chalet-inspired structure looks like a modernized old building; it only dates to 1984, the third building to house local Sons of Norway and Daughters of Norway. (The first, now Raisbeck Performance Hall, is on Walk 8.) At the lodge's east side, turn left (south) and cut through a bank parking lot to NW 56th St.

Cross a midblock crosswalk at 56th; take a marked sidewalk through another parking lot to Ballard Square (a former J. C. Penney divvied into smaller spaces). Descend the interior stairs to Ballard Square's main floor, and exit the building's south side back onto Market.

Turn right to walk east on Market. On the north side of Market at 22nd is the Ballard Building, built in 1927 to house an Eagles lodge and a silent movie theater; the stately white structure now hosts offices and a gym.

On the south side of Market at 22nd is Bergen Place park, dedicated to the neighborhood's Nordic heritage. Next to it is Vera's Restaurant, a classic breakfast and lunch diner. On the north side of Market east of 22nd are Cupcake Royale, local ground zero of the gourmet-cupcake boom, and the Majestic Bay Theater, a triplex cinema "restored" in 2000 from a 1915 neighborhood movie house. (If any of the original building remains, I can't see it.) Beyond that is a stoic 1905 library building, now home to the Kangaroo and Kiwi (the Northwest's only Australian theme bar).

East of 20th Ave. NW on the north side of Market lies the Ballard Blossom Shop with its elegant black, white, and neon facade. East of that is the Old Pequliar, an Irish pub that used to be a Swedish pub called the Valhalla. Across from there is Egan's, an intimate jazz and supper club.

At the northwest corner of 15th and Market, pay your respects to the demolished Sunset Bowl and Manning's restaurant buildings, vernacular-architecture classics that were razed for apartment behemoths. At the southeast corner of 15th and Market you can take a 15 or Rapid-Ride D bus back to your start.

This walk connects easily to two other walks. At 24th Ave. NW and NW Market St. you're 0.5 mile east of the end of Walk 16. At 14th Ave. NW and NW 46th St. you're 0.5 mile northwest of Walk 19 at the Burke-Gilman Trail and NW 43rd St.

Ballard

Points of Interest

1. **Scandinavian Specialties** 6719 15th Ave. NW, 206-784-7020, scanspecialties.com

2. **El Camion** 6416 15th Ave. NW, 206-784-5411, elcamionseattle.com

3. **St. Alphonsus Parish** 5816 15th Ave. NW, 206-784-6464, stalseattle.org

4. **Ballard Reuse** 1440 NW 52nd St., 206-297-9119, ballardreuse.com

5. **Quest Church** 1401 NW Leary Way, 206-352-3796, seattlequest.org

6. **Mike's Chili Parlor Tavern** 1447 NW Ballard Way, 206-782-2808

7. **Tractor Tavern** 5213 Ballard Ave. NW, 206-789-3599, tractortavern.com

8. **Sunset Tavern** 5433 Ballard Ave. NW, 206-784-4880, sunsettavern.com

9. **Push/Pull** 5484 Shilshole Ave. NW, 206-789-1710, pushpullseattle.weebly.com

10. **Leif Erikson Lodge** 2245 NW 57th St., 206-783-1274, leiferiksonlodge.com

23 Green Lake
Walk, Don't Run (Unless You Want To)

Above: The Green Lake Path on a quiet day

BOUNDARIES: NE Ravenna Blvd., E. Green Lake Way N., N. 77th St., and Aurora Ave. N.
DISTANCE: 4 miles
DIFFICULTY: Easy (essentially all flat)
PARKING: Metered street parking along Woodlawn
PUBLIC TRANSIT: Metro routes 26, 45, 62, and 63 stop at this walk's start.

A big spot of water and open space surrounded by North Seattle's residential calm, Green Lake got its name simply because an early surveyor noted how green it was because of algae gathering along its shallow bottom. The lake became even greener when city officials made it even shallower. Later officials have tried to make the lake less green over the years by cracking down on algae and aquatic plants, with mixed success. Through all this time, the 3-mile path around the lake's perimeter has remained a popular spot for seeing and being seen, for running, jogging, bicycling, roller skating, canoeing, swimming, and just plain walking.

Walk Description

Start at the southeast corner of NE Ravenna Blvd. and Woodlawn Ave. NE, in the east Green Lake business district. Ravenna is one of the wide boulevard streets that the Olmsted Brothers platted in 1903, running for 20 miles and connecting most of the city's major parks (Walk 11). This boulevard follows, more or less, the route of the old Ravenna Creek, which used to drain Green Lake's water into Lake Washington. To your left on Woodlawn, ❶ **Gregg's Greenlake Cycle** occupies an old building with a Spanish colonial–inspired roof. To your right is a new mixed-use complex.

Head northeast on Woodlawn past NE 71st St. On your left is ❷ **Little Red Hen,** a home for live country entertainment. Its food is as down-home as its music; there's nothing like walking the lake on a tummy full of biscuits, bacon, and gravy.

Turn left (west) on the north side of NE 72nd St. past a Nautilus gym and the Green Lake Bar and Grill. Turn right onto East Green Lake Dr. N., walking northwest three blocks, past the Seattle Public Library's stately Green Lake Branch (a twin to the University Branch, in Walk 21).

Turn left at East Green Lake and Latona Ave. NE, onto a sidewalk beside a driveway leading into Green Lake Park. The park lies mostly on land reclaimed when the lake was lowered by 7 feet in 1911, as recommended in the Olmsted Brothers' citywide park plan. It's a place of active leisure, particularly this part of it. To your left is the ❸ **Green Lake Community Center,** with a heavily used indoor pool and gym. A playground, a boat-rental shop, tennis courts, and soccer and softball fields surround it. Walk west on this sidewalk toward the lake.

Take a right turn onto the paved Green Lake Path, which curves around the lake for 3.5 miles. The inside lane of the two-lane path is reserved for walkers and runners. Cyclists and roller skaters are restricted to the one-way outside lane. If you're here on a summer weekend afternoon, you will soon learn why; traffic levels can make this path seem like a nonmotorized freeway, with sunbathers and hyperactive children as roadside distractions.

Just before you approach a small wading pool, you see a side path heading right. Turn onto this side path, out of the park and back onto East Green Lake Dr. heading west. There's a small restaurant row here.

Continue heading west on what becomes West Green Lake Dr. N. past two intersections, and then take a soft right onto Winona Ave. N. Then immediately take another soft right onto N. 77th St. for two blocks to Aurora Ave. N., part of the old Pacific Coast Highway. It's a bold-as-brass slice of the old boisterous roadside America.

Turn left (south) on Aurora's west side, past gaudy storefronts offering motorcycles, guns, used computers, and lawn mowers, as well as a couple of bars specializing in imported beers.

Keep to your proper lane on the path.

Just north of N. 73rd St. is Aurora's heart and soul, ❹ **Beth's Cafe**. Since 1954, this unreconstructed diner has served hearty portions, including the specialty 12-egg omelets, 24 hours a day.

Backtrack up Aurora and cross at the first stoplight onto Winona Ave. N., going right (east). If Beth's didn't entice your appetite, you can pick up something at the PCC Natural Market here. Continue east on Winona one block to Stone Ave. N.

Turn right (southeast) on Stone and go two blocks back to West Green Lake Dr. You're at the parking entrance to the ❺ **Seattle Public Theater**, a gorgeous 1916 bathhouse used for stage shows since the 1970s. Walk left (south) back into Green Lake Park.

Go right to rejoin the Green Lake Path, walking around the lake's west side. At the lake's southwest corner, a preserved segment of concrete grandstand seating marks the former site of the Aqua Theater, where plays and Aqua Follies musicals were held in the 1950s and 1960s. It's now the Green Lake Small Craft Center, home to youth rowing and canoeing programs.

Follow the path as it bends east, past the Pitch and Putt Golf Course, then curves northeast. As you approach the softball fields, you find a right (south) turn that takes you out of the park and back onto East Green Lake Way N.

Go left (east) on East Green Lake and continue three blocks to 4th Ave. NE and ❻ **Spud Fish & Chips** (scheduled to be rebuilt in early 2019).

Go right (southeast) on 4th one block, back to Woodlawn. Turn left (northeast) on Woodlawn and go two blocks, back to your start at Ravenna.

This walk connects easily to two other walks. It starts 0.5 mile northwest of Walk 24. On Aurora, you're a steep 0.5 mile east of Walk 20.

Points of Interest

1 **Gregg's Greenlake Cycle** 7007 Woodlawn Ave. NE, 206-523-1822, greggscycles.com

2 **Little Red Hen** 7115 Woodlawn Ave. NE, 206-522-1168, littleredhen.com

3 **Green Lake Community Center** 7201 East Green Lake Dr. N., 206-684-0780, seattle.gov/parks
/find/centers/green-lake-community-center

4 **Beth's Cafe** 7311 Aurora Ave. N., 206-782-5588, bethscafe.com

5 **Seattle Public Theater** 7312 West Green Lake Dr. N., 206-524-1300, seattlepublictheater.org

6 **Spud Fish & Chips** 6860 East Green Lake Dr. N., 206-524-0565, spudgreenlake.com

24 Ravenna and Laurelhurst
"Wilderness" and Fancy Shopping

Above: *Ravenna Park hides from the cityscape.*

BOUNDARIES: NE 65th St., NE 45th St., 30th Ave. NE, and Roosevelt Ave. NE
DISTANCE: 3 miles
DIFFICULTY: Easy (2 brief inclines)
PARKING: Free street parking along NE 65th St. and surrounding streets
PUBLIC TRANSIT: Metro routes 64, 64, 71, and 76 stop at or near this walk's start. The light-rail
   UW Station is 0.3 mile south of its end.

When you're in parts of Ravenna and Cowen Parks, you can pretend you've stepped back in
time, to when Seattle was still a tree-covered wilderness. The park's a second-growth forest;
the original trees had been cut down by the 1920s. But after nine decades, these replacement
trees have become tall, mature specimens in their own right. The park's especially grand when
you're walking along the bottom of an old glacial ravine, where the developed city disappears

from sight. The park's surrounding residential neighborhoods, traditionally home to University of Washington (UW) faculty members and other professionals, sport their own kind of spectacles, particularly at Christmastime.

Walk Description

Start on the north side of NE 65th St. at 20th Ave. NE, in front of ❶ **Third Place Books**. A well-stocked independent lit emporium, it also has a skylit café and a basement pub. Across 20th, ❷ **Gasoline Alley Antiques** is a tiny storefront crammed to the ceiling with toys, buttons, and mementos invoking several generations' childhoods.

Walk west on 65th. For the first few blocks, you are walking slightly uphill past classic Craftsman bungalows. At 15th Ave. NE you can see the stoic facade of Roosevelt High School, behind a former gas station now housing a produce stand. This street also marks the eastern boundary of the Roosevelt business district.

Turn left (south) at 65th and Roosevelt Way NE, the heart of the Roosevelt strip. Rain City Burgers is at this intersection's northwest corner, Indonesian and East Indian food spots are nearby. Besides the usual neighborhood dining and shopping opportunities, this strip has also attracted merchants selling two specific genres of goods—audio/video gear and New Age books and trinkets. Decorate your flat-screen home theater with Celtic rune stones!

Continue on Roosevelt south to NE 59th St. At this intersection's northeast corner, along the south wall of the ❸ **Trading Musician** music store, note the cute mural depicting an all-insect rock concert titled "Larvae Live!" On the southeast corner there's ❹ **Cafe Racer,** an artists hangout and watering hole. The front room features rotating exhibits by local artists. A side dining room holds a permanent kitsch painting collection called the "Official Bad Art Museum of Art."

Backtrack north on Roosevelt one block, to NE Ravenna Blvd. As mentioned in Walk 23, this is one of the Olmsted plan boulevards, wide streets with grassy median strips crossing the city. Turn right (southeast) on Ravenna for three blocks to Brooklyn Ave. NE; go left (north) on Brooklyn one block to ❺ **Cowen Park**'s west entrance. Cowen is essentially a neighborhood playground area, immediately west of the more nature-oriented **Ravenna Park.** It also has some quaint public art, such as little bronze statues of sea creatures and an oversize sundial within a grass circle.

Take the main path curving northeast and downhill to the Ravenna Park Trail. Follow the 0.5-mile main trail as it curves east, then southeast, through the bottom of the volcanic ravine alongside Ravenna Creek. At one point you're as much as 115 feet below the surrounding residential streets. At the trail's midpoint you walk under the Ravenna Park Bridge, a beautiful

Side Trip: Sand Point and the Sound Garden

If you're up to it, continue beyond this walk's official end by rejoining the Burke-Gilman Trail at the old railroad trestle above NE 45th Pl., starting east then bending north. After 2 miles of walking past impressive postwar homes and peekaboo Lake Washington views, turn right at NE 70th St. Turn left at Sand Point Way NE, then right again at NE 74th St. You're in Warren G. Magnuson Park, created from a former naval airfield. These 350 lakeside acres include trails, picnic areas, an off-leash dog park, and preserved old brick Navy buildings.

Another part of the old airfield belongs to the National Oceanic and Atmospheric Administration. This campus (open to the public weekdays) includes a public art piece comprising mounted organ pipes that generate muted tones in the wind. It's the Sound Garden, namesake of the classic Seattle rock band.

---

latticed-arch steel span that's now pedestrian only. As you gently rise back toward street level, you see a stretch of Ravenna Creek that was "daylighted" in 2006; the water had previously been diverted through underground pipes.

The park's southeast end is an open space facing NE 55th St., just west of 25th Ave. NE. From here you can walk north on 25th back to 65th St., then head west back to your start.

If you're walking this walk in December, take a brief detour west on 55th to Ravenna Ave. NE, then head north to NE Park Rd. The street annually becomes Candy Cane Lane, where every homeowner participates in elegant Christmas decorations.

If you're continuing with this walk, turn left (east) for a short uphill stretch on 55th. At the northeast corner of 55th and 25th is Kidd Valley, a venerable local family-dining spot. When it opened in the 1970s, its sign depicted a hippie chick in a halter top and cutoff jeans, leaning back on top of a giant hamburger. After citizen complaints, the image was replaced by something more abstract.

Just east of 55th and 28th Ave. NE is the Duchess Tavern, a UW student hangout dating back to the repeal era. It's full of decor celebrating UW sports over the decades. At 30th Ave. NE, the Queen Mary Tea Room is a slice of old English propriety and quiet good taste.

Turn right (south) and downhill on 30th, a narrow tree-lined residential street, along the south side of ❻ **Calvary Catholic Cemetery**. Just past the intersection with NE Blakely St., you'll see an intersection with the Burke-Gilman Trail. If you can resist the temptation to join the jogging throngs crowding this stretch of the trail from sunup to sundown, continue on 30th past NE 49th St. That's the east entrance to the ❼ **University Village** mall. It contains a bevy of major upscale chain and independent stores, ranging from Amazon Books (the e-tail giant's first brick-and-mortar site) to Zovo (a lingerie shop). It stands on what used to be the Seattle city dump, fictionalized as the setting for the local kids TV show *J. P. Patches* (Walk 19).

South of 49th, 30th Ave. curves southeast. It becomes Union Bay Place NE, an off-the-mall commercial strip where the storefronts are much more likely to be of the mom-and-pop variety. Union Bay Pl. ends at a five-way intersection with NE 45th St. and NE 45th Pl. In front of you are UW athletic fields. To your right is Burgermaster, another venerable family-dining spot. Taking a hard left onto 45th Pl., you see a short wooden railroad bridge, now part of the Burke-Gilman Trail.

On the southeast side of 45th Pl., you can take a 32 or 67 bus to the University District. Or you can walk south on 25th, which merges with Montlake Blvd. NE, to the light-rail station in front of Husky Stadium. Or you can cut across the University Village lot to 25th Ave. NE and NE 47th St. There you can take a 372 bus back to NE 65th St.

This walk connects easily with three other walks. At NE Ravenna Blvd. you're 0.5 mile north of Walks 21 and 25. At 65th and Roosevelt you're 0.5 mile southeast of Walk 23.

The 20th Ave. NE overpass is now for pedestrians and bicycles only.

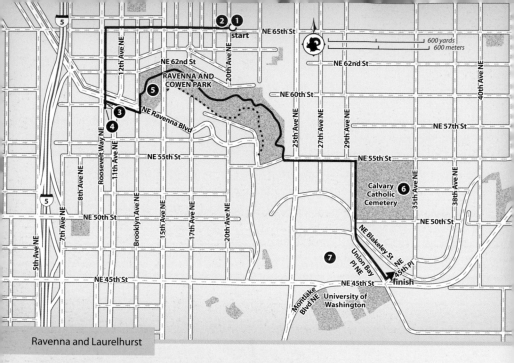

Ravenna and Laurelhurst

Points of Interest

1 **Third Place Books** 6504 20th Ave. NE, 206-525-2347, thirdplacebooks.com

2 **Gasoline Alley Antiques** 6501 20th Ave. NE, 206-524-1606, gasolinealleyantiques.com

3 **Trading Musician** 5908 Roosevelt Way NE, 206-522-6707, tradingmusician.com

4 **Cafe Racer** 5828 Roosevelt Way NE, 206-523-5282, caferacerseattle.com

5 **Cowen and Ravenna Parks** 5849 15th Ave. NE, 206-684-4075, seattle.gov/parks/find/parks /cowen-park and seattle.gov/parks/find/parks/ravenna-park

6 **Calvary Catholic Cemetery** 5041 35th Ave. NE, 206-522-0996

7 **University Village** 2623 NE University Village St., 206-523-0622, uvillage.com

25 The U District and University of Washington Campus A Class Act

Above: Denny Hall, the oldest building on the UW campus

BOUNDARIES: NE 50th St., Montlake Blvd. NE, NE Boat St., and 5th Ave. NE
DISTANCE: 4.25 miles, in 2 segments
DIFFICULTY: Moderate (a slight incline at the start)
PARKING: Free street parking west of Roosevelt Way NE; metered street parking on and
    east of Roosevelt
PUBLIC TRANSIT: A dozen Metro routes stop near this walk's start; light-rail UW Station
    in front of Husky Stadium

The University of Washington (UW) is the biggest single college campus west of the Rockies—and one of the handsomest in the United States. It's a place of stunning structures amid landscaped repose, designed around a sweeping view of Mount Rainier. From Greek Row to the Liberal Arts Quadrangle (Quad) to the Health Sciences Center, its major buildings present a thorough retrospective of late-19th- and 20th-century institutional architecture. Adjacent to the campus, and somewhat grungier looking, is the first Seattle neighborhood for thousands who arrived as students and remained in town. Its main retail strip is also the main off-campus retail strip, where you can spot students from around the world and hipster youths from around the metro area.

Walk Description

Start at the north side of NE 40th St. and 9th Ave. NE, at the University Friends Meeting, a Quaker church with a clean minimalist look. One of its longtime members, naturalist and political activist Floyd Schmoe, led a drive in the 1990s to remake the vacant lot across 40th into ❶ **Peace Park**. Its centerpiece is a statue of Sadako Sasaki, a 12-year-old victim of the Hiroshima blast. She's depicted holding a paper crane, as part of a healing ritual.

Walk east on 40th, under the University Bridge and past a new subcampus of dormitory towers. At 40th and Brooklyn Ave. NE, the gently angular UW Ethnic Cultural Center faces the older concrete box of the Ethnic Cultural Theater.

Turn left onto University Way NE. Everyone calls it The Ave. It starts with the Tudor-style ❷ **College Inn** building. Built in 1909, it's now a European-style hotel with a pub in the basement and shops on street level. At the southwest corner of 41st and The Ave., the UW's ❸ **Jones Playhouse** preserves the 1931 facade of the old Seattle Repertory Playhouse.

The Ave.'s retail and restaurant row really starts north of 41st, with the Big Time brewpub and Shultzy's Sausage. Above 42nd, Bulldog News has periodicals from the world over, on real paper. At 43rd, the bistro Flowers recycles the cursive neon from a florist shop. The next block up, the Varsity Cinema's flashy marquee faces the ❹ **University Book Store**, the district's retail anchor. Besides books, it has computers, art supplies, clothes, Husky logo trinkets, and CDs. The latter makes it one of the last of the district's once-numerous record shops.

Turn left (west) onto the south side of NE 45th St., and head toward another classic movie house, the Neptune (now a concert venue). Across Brooklyn Ave. NE, the UW has taken over Safeco Insurance's former 22-story office tower. Across 45th from there is a snazzier high-rise, the Art Deco Deca (née Edmond Meany) Hotel, where every room is a corner room.

Return to University Way and turn left to resume heading north. At the northeast corner of 45th and The Ave., classical terra-cotta covers the 1913 Wells Fargo (formerly University State) Bank building. The storefronts north of that are dominated by young-adult apparel and eats. There's also a pulsating street life, involving student-age folk in most every fashion style of the past three decades.

Take a right onto the south side of NE 50th St. A short flight of steps leads to the Grand Illusion, a 49-seat movie theater on the second floor of a tiny retail building. In the 1970s, Seattle's reputation as an art-film-going town began here. If you'd like to stop now, you can catch a south-bound bus at the southwest corner of 50th and The Ave.

Still with us? Then continue east on 50th, past some big churches—University Christian, University Lutheran, Hillel House, and the evangelical Churchome. The latter is in a brick former Christian Science church at 17th Ave. NE and 50th.

Turn right (south) on 17th, better known as Greek Row. It's a wide boulevard with a grassy median strip and big trees shading the fraternities and sororities. Cross 45th and enter the UW campus, where 17th becomes Memorial Way.

To your right, the first campus building you see is the ❺ **Burke Museum of Natural History and Culture**. This trove of regional artifacts is the state's oldest museum, founded in 1885; the current building dates to 1962 but will be razed after an adjacent new building opens in 2019. Cross Memorial to the back of the Jacobsen Observatory, whose original 1895 telescope still watches the skies. Across a parking lot from the observatory's front side, the Hughes Penthouse Theatre is the oldest theater-in-the-round auditorium in the United States.

Walk south from the observatory. Take the first left turn, onto Stevens Way. It curves south-east, past Hutchinson Hall, one of the campus's Gothic palaces. Built in the 1920s for women's

Theodor Jacobsen Observatory, the campus's second-oldest building

athletics, it now houses the drama department. Farther down are Lewis and Clark Halls, 1900-era brick fortresses built as the university's first dorms.

Take a right turn at Clark Hall, onto Skagit Lane. To your right is the Music Building, part of the Liberal Arts Quadrangle. You might hear singers and pianists practicing in its studios. To your left is the Communications Building, where mass media is still taught as a paying profession. Next to it is Thomson Hall, with a bust in front honoring Sen. Henry "Scoop" Jackson, who funneled much federal research money to the UW. Its School of International Studies, based at Thomson, is now named for Jackson. Beyond that is the Grieg Garden, a former parking lot reclaimed as green space, surrounding a statue of the Norwegian composer.

Turn right at Thomson Hall onto King Lane, walking northwest through the Quad, a rectangular lawn surrounded by seven spectacular Gothic buildings. It's especially striking during cherry blossom season. Continue past the Quad toward Denny Hall. The campus's oldest building (1895) looks like a limestone French château.

Take a left at Denny Hall toward the red Romanesque Parrington Hall. Continue southwest from Parrington on George Washington Lane, which curves south at the ➏ **Henry Art Gallery,** a top contemporary exhibition center. Across the lane, the ➐ **UW Visitors Center** is on the lower level of Odegaard Undergraduate Library (a 1960s brutalist box known on campus as UGL-Y).

Turn left (east) past a George Washington statue, up some wide stairs, and across the brick-paved Red Square (nobody calls it by its official name, Central Plaza) to ➑ **Suzzallo Library,** the grandest yet most inviting of the UW's Gothic marvels. If the library's open, go in and see its magnificent lobby and grand staircase, leading to the spectacular Graduate Reading Room.

From Suzzallo's south side (with Gerberding Hall's churchlike bell tower to your right), head right (southeast) to Drumheller Fountain, also known as Frosh Pond. The shallow pool was the center point of the Alaska-Yukon-Pacific Exposition, a fair staged in 1909 to celebrate Seattle's arrival as a trade center. Walk around to Garfield Lane, in front of the Chemistry Building on the pond's southwest side.

Take Garfield southwest to the Medicinal Herb Garden, a secluded green space with dozens of plant samples to observe but not touch.

Turn left (east) on Stevens Way, across the Rainier Vista promenade, named for the mountain you'll see if it's nice out. Just east of that is the Sylvan Theater, a secluded green space with four Doric columns from the UW's original downtown building.

Turn east on Snohomish Way, onto the Burke-Gilman Trail. From here you can look across a skybridge toward Husky basketball's home, ➒ **Hec Edmundson Pavilion**. (Nobody calls it by its official name, Alaska Airlines Arena.)

Murals at the light-rail station near Husky Stadium

Turn right onto the Burke-Gilman, curving southwest. Try not to get run over by jogging ROTC squads while you look east toward Husky Stadium, home of the again-mighty UW football program. In front of the stadium is the light-rail ❿ **UW Station**; etched-glass murals along its steep escalators depict local sea life.

Just past the Triangle Parking Garage, take a side path down to NE Pacific St.; cross Pacific and walk southeast to the ⓫ **UW Medical Center**'s main entrance. Enter the medical center. Take a right turn at the lobby, through the main corridor with its impressive public art collection, toward a big sign reading PACIFIC ELEVATORS. Descend to level 1. Follow the signs to the Plaza Cafe; cut through the dining area and out the building's south side.

Head right (southwest) on Columbia Road, which becomes NE Boat St., hugging the Montlake Cut's north shore. You might glimpse a rowing practice or a UW oceanography lab boat.

At the end of Boat St. turn left (west) back onto Pacific, which becomes NE Northlake Way. Continue west on Northlake under the University Bridge and the I-5 Ship Canal Bridge. On Northlake's north side are two acclaimed eateries, Voula's Offshore Cafe and Northlake Tavern and Pizza. On Northlake's south side at 5th Ave. NE are a small waterfront park and ⓬ **Ivar's Salmon House**, designed to look like an American Indian longhouse.

To return to your start, backtrack to Pacific and 7th Ave. NE. Go left (north) on 7th; take the outdoor steps up to 40th St.

This walk connects easily with four other walks. It ends 0.75 mile northeast of Walk 19's end and starts across the University Bridge from Walk 27's end. At 45th and University Way you're four blocks west of Walk 21. At 50th and University Way you're 0.5 mile south of Walk 24.

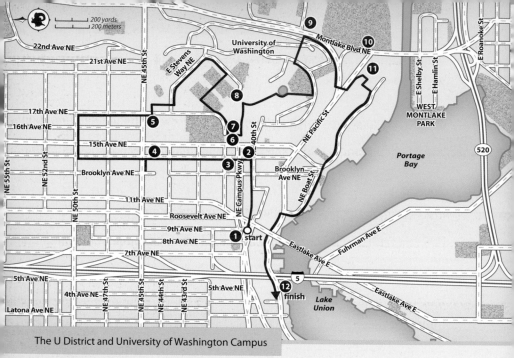

Points of Interest

1. **Peace Park** NE 40th St. and 9th Ave. NE, seattle.gov/parks/find/parks/peace-park

2. **College Inn** 4000 University Way NE, 206-633-4441, collegeinnseattle.com

3. **Jones Playhouse** 4045 University Way NE, 206-543-5140, drama.washington.edu/facilities
/floyd-and-delores-jones-playhouse

4. **University Book Store** 4326 University Way NE, 206-634-4300, ubookstore.com

5. **Burke Museum of Natural History and Culture** NE 45th St. and 17th Ave. NE, 206-543-7907,
burkemuseum.org

6. **Henry Art Gallery** 15th Ave. NE and NE 41st St., 206-543-2280, henryart.org

7. **University of Washington Visitors Center** 4060 George Washington Lane, 206-543-9198,
washington.edu/visit

8. **Suzzallo Library** UW Central Plaza, 206-543-0242, lib.washington.edu/suzzallo

9. **Hec Edmundson Pavilion** 3870 Montlake Blvd. NE, 206-543-2210, gohuskies.com

10. **UW Station** 3720 Montlake Blvd. E., soundtransit.org

11. **UW Medical Center** 1959 NE Pacific St., 206-598-3300, uwmedicine.org/uw-medical-center

12. **Ivar's Salmon House** 401 NE Northlake Way, 206-632-0767, ivars.com

26 Foster Island and the Arboretum
In the Trees

BOUNDARIES: 24th Ave. E., E. Hamlin St., Arboretum Dr. E., and Lake Washington Blvd. E.
DISTANCE: 4.5 miles
DIFFICULTY: Easy (1 gentle incline)
PARKING: Limited street parking (except on UW football game days); free parking in 2 Arboretum lots.
PUBLIC TRANSIT: Metro routes 43 and 48 stop near this walk's start; light-rail UW Station is just
   north of the Montlake Bridge.

The City of Seattle and the University of Washington (UW) jointly run the Washington Park Arboretum, a 230-acre plant museum disguised as a nature corridor and a popular get-away-from-it-all spot. You don't need to be a scholar of plant science to enjoy it; you just need a curious mind and an attentive eye. This route takes you into the arboretum via a unique walk along the water, through a pair of artificial islets. At the heart of your walk are two beautifully meditative areas, an elaborate Japanese garden and an open meadow honoring the Pacific Rim's diverse flora.

Walk Description

Start at the southeast side of the Montlake drawbridge. There are steps down to a pedestrian path along the Montlake Cut's southern concrete wall, regularly repainted with graffiti promoting UW rowing. Turn right to walk east along this waterside trail. At a sign reading ARBORETUM WATERFRONT TRAIL, turn right.

Follow the trail through East Montlake Park to the Marsh Island footbridge. (Note: This part of the walk is occasionally closed due to construction work on the WA 520 bridge or high-water conditions. It can also be very muddy in spots during the rainy season.)

Much of the following path is on a boardwalk, or floating trail. It winds east through, well, marshes, with plenty of nesting birds (wrens and blackbirds in summer, crows in winter). This little piece of nature was transformed from shallow waters to a flat islet in the early 20th century, when Lake Washington and Lake Union were lowered several feet.

Take the trail across another wooden bridge and onto the larger Foster Island. This bridge and the subsequent stretch of boardwalk along Foster's north side offer great water-level views of Union Bay. You can see pleasure boats, canoes, rowing crews, and waterfowl; in the distance are Husky Stadium and the upscale Laurelhurst neighborhood. The boardwalk becomes a dirt trail, which leads to a crossroads. Turn right.

Follow this path south under the WA 520 freeway and into the ❶ **Washington Park Arboretum.** This area of bending creeks and tiny islets is popular with canoeists; you can become one temporarily by renting from the ❷ **UW Waterfront Activities Center**, located near the stadium.

One short footbridge later, you're off Foster Island and back on the mainland. The trail soon leads to a paved street, Broadmoor Dr. E. To your left you can peer in at the private Broadmoor Golf Club. Beyond that you might see some mansion roofs from the gated Broadmoor residential community.

Turn left onto Arboretum Dr. E. To your left you soon see the Graham Visitors Center, where you can get a detailed map of the arboretum and all its plant and tree samples. A greenhouse complex is just south of that. From this point, the road becomes pedestrian only, winding gently uphill. Despite this area's natural appearance, it was completely logged in the late 19th century by the Puget Mill Company. The City of Seattle acquired the land in 1900. In 1934 the city brought in UW as its partner in developing the arboretum, with the help of Works Progress Administration (WPA) laborers.

Continue strolling along Arboretum Dr. You catch occasional glimpses of the private golf course behind the fence to your left. In closer view, you see displays of Japanese and Asiatic maples, magnolias, mountain ashes, birches, poplars, legumes, camellias, rhododendrons, and witch hazel plants. More than 12,000 plants are in the arboretum's official collection.

Eventually you reach a clearing to your right, the Pacific Connections Meadow, the arboretum's newest attraction, which features a circular gravel path. Take a right turn onto the circle, going counterclockwise. Surrounding it are gardens representing different Pacific Rim places: Australia, New Zealand, China, Chile, and Cascadia (the United States and Canadian Northwest).

Just before the circle returns to Arboretum Dr., take a right onto the Cascadia Forest Trail. It wends a very indirect path through locally native trees and plants and leads to stone-paved steps, switchbacking downhill.

At the bottom of this trail, take a right turn back onto Arboretum Dr. To your left you find a WPA-built stone cottage that serves as both a symbolic gatehouse and a residence for the park's security chief. From here, you can continue on Arboretum Dr. out of the park and onto the Madison Valley retail strip.

If you're continuing with us, take a sharp right turn onto Lake Washington Blvd. E. On your left, you soon see the ❸ **Seattle Japanese Garden**. Since 1960 this exquisite formal garden has entranced and relaxed thousands with its artfully placed ponds, paths, bridges, lanterns, shrubs, and flowers. The garden has a $6 adult admission fee ($4 for kids, seniors, and the disabled; free for children 5 and under). It's closed in winter.

North of the Japanese Garden on Lake Washington Blvd., take a right turn onto a short parking strip that leads to Azalea Way. Wind north on Azalea. In some stretches, it's a gravel path. In others, it's a wide grassy promenade. Those parts can be muddy during and after long rains. Along both sides are many more tree and plant samples, identified with handy signs. The tree samples alone include the holly, ash, walnut, hawthorne, and (yes, Monty Python viewers) the larch.

Azalea eventually leads to a crossroads, where you can see the visitors center to your right. Take a left instead. Cross the Wilcox Footbridge, a narrow concrete-and-brick archway over Lake Washington Blvd. It looks fancier than a pedestrian overpass needs to be for a reason. An aboveground sewer pipe is hidden inside all that stonework. Head west and out of the arboretum.

Continue west on E. Lynn St. back to 24th. There's a little retail strip with a coffeehouse, a convenience store, a couple of moderately priced restaurants, and a cute antiques and curio shop. You can take a right up 24th back to your start or take a 43 or 48 bus.

This walk connects easily with three other walks. It starts 0.75 mile south of Walk 25, across the Montlake Bridge. It ends 0.25 mile north of Walk 27. At Arboretum Dr. and Lake Washington Blvd. you're 0.5 mile southwest of Walk 28.

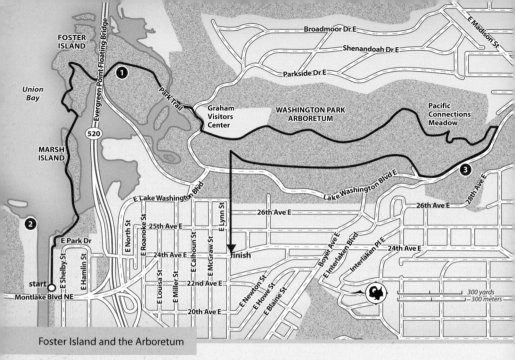

Foster Island and the Arboretum

Points of Interest

1 **Washington Park Arboretum** 2300 Arboretum Dr. E., 206-543-8800, botanicgardens.uw.edu /washington-park-arboretum

2 **UW Waterfront Activities Center** 3710 Montlake Blvd. NE, 206-534-9433, washington.edu /ima/waterfront

3 **Seattle Japanese Garden** 1075 Lake Washington Blvd. E., 206-684-4725, seattlejapanesegarden.org

27 Interlaken and Montlake
Natural Curves

Above: St. Demetrios Greek Orthodox Church

BOUNDARIES: 10th Ave. E., E. Interlaken Blvd., 24th Ave. E., Boyer Ave. E., and Eastlake Ave. E.
DISTANCE: 3.5 miles
DIFFICULTY: Easy (mostly flat or downhill)
PARKING: Free street parking on 10th Ave. E. (north of E. Roanoke St.)
PUBLIC TRANSIT: Metro route 49 stops near this walk's start.

Interlaken Blvd. is one of the Olmsted plan's (Walk 11) promenades through the city. Before that, in the 1890s, it was part of a bicycle-path network that crossed Seattle in the pre–Model T years. It remains a great place to retreat from the big city and commune with the big trees. Like Ravenna Park (Walk 24), Interlaken lets you pretend you're out in a deep wilderness, without the wasteful fuel consumption of a real country road trip. Beneath this path, the Montlake neighborhood sports some modestly sized but stately homes, and one grand mid-century modern church.

Walk Description

Start at E. Roanoke St., going east from 10th Ave. E. Pass the south end of ❶ **Roanoke Park,** a nice little neighborhood green space.

Turn right (southeast) onto Delmar Dr. E. After you cross an overpass above WA 520, you get a peek to your right of Seattle Prep, a Jesuit high school with a 1950s-modern look.

Take a soft right onto E. Interlaken Blvd. You're immediately twisting your way through ❷ **Interlaken Park**. You're walking up, then down Capitol Hill's steep northeast slope. Tall trees on either side of this narrow, curving street block most views of anything beyond them. Some of these second-growth trees are up to a century old. There are even a few old-growth redwoods in the mix. It all makes for a spectacular interplay of light and shadow, especially on a sunny late afternoon. Cars are allowed on this part of the boulevard, but you won't see many of them. As the road U-turns north, you find a small plaque mounted on a rock to your right that honors Louisa Boren Denny, one of Seattle's founding white settlers.

Shortly after, the boulevard forks with Interlaken Dr. E. Take a left to continue on E. Interlaken Blvd. After another U-turn south, there's an intersection with 19th Ave. E. Cars have to turn onto 19th, but you can keep going straight as the boulevard becomes restricted to pedestrians and bicycles. Along this 0.5-mile stretch you can more clearly hear the birds and feel one with the flora and fauna. Reality intrudes at an intersection with 21st Ave. E., as cars rejoin you on the boulevard. Soon after that you're heading out of the park and back into civilization.

A side path from Interlaken Blvd.

Turn left (north) onto 24th Ave. E; then immediately turn left (northwest) onto Boyer Ave. E. To your right you soon spot Boyer Children's Clinic, providing both therapy and schooling to kids with neuromuscular disorders. The handsome 1991 brick structure includes some nice public art and signs done up in a grown-up designer's idea of kids' handwriting.

Two residential blocks later, dogleg right onto 22nd Ave. E., for the first of two digressions off Boyer. Take an immediate left onto E. Blaine St. The homes here take on a storybook feel. Mostly built in the late 1920s, they range from English cottages to Tudor A-frames. Blaine ends at 19th Ave. E., with the grand dome and cupola of ❸ **St. Demetrios Greek Orthodox Church.** Built in 1962, the modern yet traditional building was designed by Paul Thiry, one of the chief architects of the Seattle World's Fair. Take a left-right dogleg around the church and back onto Boyer.

Resume going northwest on Boyer to 16th Ave. E., where you make your second digression. Heading right (north) on 16th, you see some more exquisite brick Tudor homes. Then 16th ends at E. Calhoun St., by the ❹ **Montlake Playground and Community Center.** The latter occupies two buildings. The older building is an extralarge version of the Tudor cottage architecture you've already seen in the neighborhood.

Turn left (west) on Calhoun, which quickly becomes a pedestrian-only path. Turn left (south) on 15th Ave. E. and go one block, back to Boyer. Take a right to resume going northwest on Boyer's north side, under WA 520. Interspersed among the tasteful old homes here are some boxy new townhomes.

As Boyer curves from northwest to north, the ❺ **Queen City Yacht Club** shows up on your right. The long, low clubhouse you see from the street extends for two more stories below. The members-only moorage slips can accommodate more than 200 boats. The club sponsors a parade of lighted boats around Seattle's waterways every Christmas season.

Continue as Boyer bends northwest again, becoming Fuhrman Ave. E. You get glimpses of Portage Bay and the Montlake Cut between houses. Just before the intersection with Eastlake Ave. E. at the south end of the University Bridge, to your left, is a Tudor-style minicastle. It's now the Polish-style ❻ **Sebi's Bistro**; its former identities include Scoundrel's Lair, Rapunzel's, and the Llahngaelhyn (a 1960s jazz club). Just beyond Eastlake to your right is the ❼ **Pocock Rowing Center**, the region's top rowing club and school.

Turn left (southwest) onto the east side of Eastlake and go one block, past the artisan bakery Le Fournil. Then take a soft left onto Harvard Ave. E. From here you can take a 0.5-mile uphill trek back to Roanoke Ave.

The walk connects easily with three other walks. It starts five blocks east of Walk 9. Its midpoint is three blocks north of Walk 26's end. It ends across the University Bridge from Walk 25's start.

Interlaken and Montlake

Points of Interest

① Roanoke Park 950 E. Roanoke St., 206-684-4075, seattle.gov/parks/find/parks/roanoke-park

② Interlaken Park 2451 Delmar Ave. E., seattle.gov/parks/find/parks/interlaken-park

③ St. Demetrios Greek Orthodox Church 2100 Boyer Ave. E., 206-631-2500, saintdemetrios.com

④ Montlake Playground and Community Center 1618 E. Calhoun St., 206-684-4736, seattle.gov/parks/find/centers/montlake-community-center

⑤ Queen City Yacht Club 2608 Boyer Ave. E., 206-709-2000, queencity.org

⑥ Sebi's Bistro 3242 Eastlake Ave. E., 206-420-2199, sebisbistro.com

⑦ Pocock Rowing Center 3320 Fuhrman Ave. E., 206-328-0778, pocockrowingcenter.org

28 Madrona and Madison Park
Lakeside Leisure

Above: *The Walker-Ames House, residence of the University of Washington president*

BOUNDARIES: 34th Ave. E., E. Union St., 43rd Ave. E., and E. Madison St.
DISTANCE: 3.75 miles, in 2 segments
DIFFICULTY: Moderate (1 rather long uphill stretch)
PARKING: Free parking on 34th Ave. E. and adjoining streets
PUBLIC TRANSIT: Metro routes 2 and 3 stop near this walk's start.

Seattle's eastern slopes overlooking Lake Washington contain some of the city's grandest residences. This portion of the lakefront and vicinity also offers big and small parks, a pioneers' meeting hall, gay and lesbian sunbathers, and Seattle's only (unofficial) Kurt Cobain memorial. Your walk starts amid some popular bistros, then follows a narrow wooden bridge over a ravine. At its middle is Madison Park, a former enclave of summer cottages that's now a self-contained town within the city.

Walk Description

Start at 34th Ave. and E. Union St., center of the Madrona business district. It has a handful of quaint, comfy eateries. One favorite is the ❶ **Hi-Spot Café,** a breakfast and lunch place in a 1904 Victorian home. Weekend brunch lines here often stretch onto the sidewalk. Walk north on 34th two blocks to E. Pine St.

Turn right (east) on Pine, past some classic upper-middle-class housing stock. Continue as Pine becomes a pedestrian-only path for three blocks, alternating between sidewalks and down-hill stairs between some dense trees, to Madrona Dr.

On the east side of Madrona Dr., Pine turns into a wooden pedestrian bridge over a deep, lush ravine. It's reminiscent of the trestles that once bore trolley cars rattling down to Lake Washington. This bridge has a turnoff in the middle, a secondary bridge leading left. But keep going straight, to Pine and Evergreen Pl. There's a light pole right in the middle of your way at the bridge's east end, which helps discourage motorcyclists from crossing it.

Wind left (north) on Evergreen, which is barely wider than an alley. In two blocks it widens (slightly) into 39th Ave. E. Dense trees and shrubbery surround it, hiding the homes of the affluent and reclusive. One of these, to your right, is the former home of Starbucks boss Howard Schultz. You can tell it by the private driveway he had added, which cuts through the city-owned ❷ **Viretta Park.**

Enter Viretta, descend some stairs, and go right (east) through the small neighborhood park. Near its center is an ordinary wood-and-metal bench covered in etched graffiti and often adorned with flowers. This is Kurt's Bench, still a gathering place for fans of singer-songwriter Kurt Cobain. On the day in 1994 when Cobain's death was announced, this spot was the closest the public could get to the garage (since demolished) where he'd died. These fans have unofficially nicknamed the space Kurt's Park.

From Viretta's eastern end, head left (north) along Lake Washington Blvd. To your right is the entrance to another small park, ❸ **Denny-Blaine.** It's a grassy strip that leads to a short public (and unofficially topless) beach. Just north of Denny-Blaine is a five-way intersection. Take a soft right onto McGilvra Blvd. E., winding north. The lakefront along this stretch is all private. You can see massive homes with views to your left, and old mansions and newer McMansions (or peeka-boo pieces of them, or just their garages) to your right.

McGilvra curves northeast, then north again as it passes the quite exclusive Seattle Tennis Club. It's said to have a decade-long waiting list for membership. North of there, McGilvra traverses inland blocks, without views and with significantly smaller houses. Some of these lots were orig-inally platted as summer homes for the affluent.

Turn right (east) at E. Garfield St. and go three blocks. On the southeast side of Garfield and 42nd Ave. E., a fence encloses but doesn't conceal a little private residential enclave. It was originally the estate of Judge John McGilvra, one of the neighborhood's initial developers. During the Great Depression, its then owners turned it into a small gated community, with several smaller homes in place of McGilvra's mansion.

Turn left (north) on 43rd Ave. E. To your right, three residential towers stand on the site of an old amusement pier Judge McGilvra had built to stimulate land sales in the neighborhood. North of those is the brick facade of ❹ **Washington Pioneer Hall,** home for a century to the Pioneer Association of the State of Washington. North of that lies ❺ **Madison Park** itself, a stretch of lakefront that McGilvra donated to the city as a public amenity for residents of his developments.

Take a hard left onto E. Madison St., heading southwest through the Madison Park business strip. It's a pleasant stroll past sidewalk cafés, fashionable boutiques, and even a few practical

Kurt's Bench in Viretta Park, where fans pay tribute to musician Kurt Cobain

places like a small supermarket and a hardware store. One of the oldest spots here is the **6** **Red Onion Tavern,** a cozy bar with crimson wallpaper, a fireplace, and hearty pizzas.

Continue southwest on Madison beyond the business district, heading uphill past some very fancy homes. The fanciest is the **7** **Samuel Hyde House,** a brick edifice with a white Corinthian portico. It's now the Russian consul general's residence (or was, until the Seattle Russian consulate closed in early 2018). Beyond it stand the wrought-iron fences surrounding Broadmoor, the city's oldest and poshest gated development. Near 36th Ave. E. you see a fancy brick bus shelter, built by Broadmoor for its residents' household staffs, outside the fence.

Turn left (south) on 36th, continuing uphill. To your immediate right is the **8** **Pantages Mansion.** Built in 1909 by a vaudeville-theater mogul, it has two stories of white plaster beneath a red-tile roof. Three blocks later, at the northeast corner of 36th and E. Valley St., is the big brick Walker-Ames House, official residence of the UW president. After crossing E. Mercer St., 36th transforms from a wide landscaped boulevard into a one-lane side street, winding downhill toward Lake Washington Blvd. E.

Turn southeast on Lake Washington Blvd. and continue one block. To your left you see a 1917 Tudor mansion behind a short uphill driveway. It's part of the Bush School, a K–12 private academy.

Take a right onto 37th Ave. E., which curves southeast and becomes Dorffel Dr. E., another narrow tree-lined street. You see other historic houses, as well as brief glimpses of the lake views these houses were built to exploit. When it forks with E. John St., keep right to stay on Dorffel.

Then take the next right fork, going southwest onto Maiden Lane E. for one block, back to Madrona Dr. Turn right on Madrona. To your left you see the sprawling **9** **Epiphany Parish of Seattle.** Noted local architect Ellsworth Storey designed the Episcopal church's chapel (its easternmost building) in 1911. To your right you see another spectacular brick bus shelter, a remnant from the prewar trolley days. Here you can catch a 2 bus back to 34th and Union.

This walk connects easily to two other walks. At 36th and Madison you're 0.5 mile northeast of Walk 26. At Pine and Madrona Dr. you're 1 mile north of Walk 31.

Lake Washington

MADISON PARK ❹
3rd Ave E
❻ ❺
E Garfield St
E Newton St
McGilvra Blvd E

DENNY-BLAINE PARK ❸

Lake Washington Blvd E Pine St
footbridge

39th Ave E
VIRETTA PARK ❷
Madrona Dr
MADRONA PARK
38th Ave E ─ Walker-Ames House
LAKEVIEW PARK
38th Ave E
❼
37th Ave E
finish ❾
37th Ave E
❽ 36th Ave E
36th Ave E
Broadmoor Dr E
34th Ave E
35th Ave E
Shenandoah Dr E
33rd Ave E
❶ start
Parkside Dr E
Lake Washington Blvd
34th Ave E
33rd Ave E
E Madison St
32nd Ave E
WASHINGTON PARK ARBORETUM
E Republican St
E Harrison St
31st Ave E
30th Ave E
E Pine St
E Union St

Martin Luther King Jr Way

Madrona and Madison Park

200 yards
200 meters

Points of Interest

❶ **Hi-Spot Café** 1410 34th Ave., 206-325-7905, hispotcafe.com

❷ **Viretta Park** 151 Lake Washington Blvd. E., 206-684-4075, seattle.gov/parks/find/parks/viretta-park

❸ **Denny-Blaine Park** 200 Lake Washington Blvd. E., 206-684-4075, seattle.gov/parks/find/parks /denny-blaine-park

❹ **Washington Pioneer Hall** 1642 43rd Ave., 206-325-0888, wapioneers.org

❺ **Madison Park** E. Madison St. and E. Howe St., seattle.gov/parks/find/parks/madison-park

❻ **Red Onion Tavern** 4210 E. Madison St., 206-323-1611

❼ **Samuel Hyde House** 3726 E. Madison St.

❽ **Pantages Mansion** 1117 36th Ave. E.

❾ **Epiphany Parish of Seattle** 1805 38th Ave., 206-324-2573, epiphanyseattle.org

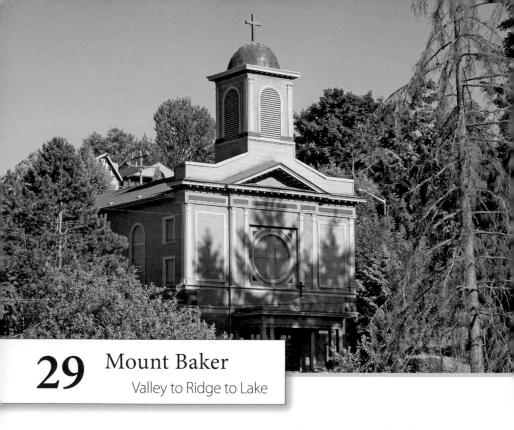

29 Mount Baker
Valley to Ridge to Lake

Above: *Our Lady of Mount Virgin Church*

BOUNDARIES: Sound Transit Mount Baker Station at Rainier Ave. S. and Martin Luther King Jr. Way S.;
Sam Smith Park at 29th Ave. S. and S. Atlantic St.; Lakeside Ave. S.; 18th Ave. S.
DISTANCE: 4 miles
DIFFICULTY: Challenging (1 steep, but brief, segment)
PARKING: Free or metered parking along side streets facing Rainier Ave.
PUBLIC TRANSIT: Light-rail Mount Baker Station; 8 Metro routes at the nearby Mount Baker
Transit Center

Rainier Valley ("The Valley," in local lore) is where ethnic communities from Italian to Laotian have set-tled at various times. It lies between Beacon Hill and Mount Baker Ridge, the site of many old money manses west of Lake Washington. The Valley's main drag, Rainier Ave., is set at a northwest-southeast angle to give a view of the mountain on clear days.

Walk Description

Start at Rainier Ave. S. and Martin Luther King Jr. Way S., at the base of the light-rail ❶ **Mount Baker Station.** Head northwest (left) along the east side of Rainier.

Enter the grounds of the Lowe's (formerly Eagle) hardware store. At its front entrance you'll find a small shrine to the block's former occupant, Sick's Seattle Stadium. Still mourned by local old-timers, it was home to baseball's minor-league Rainiers (yes, named for the beer) and the one-season major-league Pilots.

Cut across the Lowe's parking lot to its northeast exit. Turn right on S. Bayview St., then left onto Martin Luther King Jr. Way S. You're passing the ❷ **MLK Jr. Memorial Park,** a tall cylindrical monument surrounded by concentric paths and terraces.

Turn west (left) onto S. Walker St. At 25th Ave. S. you'll spot Green Plate Special, a garden and learning center teaching middle schoolers about plants and the origins of food. At 24th, the 2100 Building includes a ❸ **FareStart Café** (part of a nonprofit that trains people in food-service careers) and an off-kilter window treatment at its top.

Cross Rainier at Walker and head southeast (left). You'll soon spot ❹ **Borracchini's Bakery and Deli,** one of the last remnants of the old Garlic Gulch Italian American neighborhood. It's a great place for sandwiches, pastries, custom cakes, and much more.

Head back onto the west side of Rainier, going northwest. You'll pass a cool used-furniture storefront, a barn-shaped lumber store, a teriyaki joint, and the outlet store for ("Oh Boy!") ❺ **Oberto Sausage Factory Store and Deli.**

Beyond S. Massachusetts St. and just before a freeway overpass, take a left turn onto a paved foot/bike path. Three blocks later, at the foot of 18th Ave. S., take two right turns onto the I-90 Trail heading east. When you reach the overpass again, look southeast down Rainier. Maybe you'll see the mountain; maybe you won't.

Continue as the trail separates from the freeway, overlooking the Atlantic Street Center (a youth-services agency in a handsome old brick building).

The trail bends north at the Benvenuto Viewpoint, where you can catch a good glimpse of the downtown skyline. Keep going north until you find a crosswalk traversing 23rd Ave. S. Turn right across it.

Take another right, past the magnificent former Concord Elementary School, now the ❻ **Northwest African American Museum.** To your left, you'll see a sculpture of an abstract butterfly. It's the centerpiece of ❼ **Jimi Hendrix Park,** the newest and biggest of Seattle's many tributes to the acid-rock legend. Turn left onto a paved path around the statue, onto a stretch of park built on a lid over the freeway.

Turn south (right) onto MLK Way. To your right, Blue Dog Pond isn't a pond, but it is a fenced, dog-friendly park with cute 2-D dog sculptures. To your left, ❽ **Our Lady of Mount Virgin Parish** is a stoic hillside sanctuary, now performing mass in several immigrant-community languages.

Cross MLK Way at S. Massachusetts St., turn north (left), and reenter Sam Smith Park. Turn east (right) back onto the I-90 Trail. This stretch of it is adorned with pairs of words etched into the pavement (TWILIGHT/DAWN, ABOVE/BELOW, and so on) and small square monuments with pithy quotations. It leads into the bike/pedestrian tunnel underneath Mount Baker Ridge. You can take this tunnel 0.25 mile to Lake Washington and the end of Walk 31.

If you're still with us: just before the tunnel entrance, turn south (right) past some tennis courts and out of the park, to 29th Ave. S. and S. Atlantic St.

Downtown skyline from the Mount Baker Ridge Viewpoint

Turn south on 29th. It's quite steep, but only for about 500 feet. The slope eases up once you get to ❾ **Bradner Gardens Park,** a recently installed showcase for many types of urban gardening.

Turn west (left) onto S. Grand St. and go two gently uphill blocks, to 31st Ave. S. If you have time, turn north (left) and walk two and a half blocks to the ❿ **Mount Baker Ridge Viewpoint.** Besides a stunning city view, it has embedded stones through which sunset light directly passes on each solstice and equinox.

Head back south on the west side of 31st to S. Walker St. On the northwest corner of this intersection, the landmark Charles P. Dose House was built in a modern English style in 1910 by one of the neighborhood's first residential developers.

Cross Walker and then turn east (left) along the south side of Walker, which becomes Dose Terrace S., past two square brick gateposts. The next four downhill blocks feature equally large, showy houses from the early 20th century.

At the end of Dose Terrace is an outdoor staircase. Descend the 120 concrete steps to Lake Washington Blvd. S. and Mount Baker Beach.

Turn south (right) onto Lake Washington Blvd., to the intersection with Lake Park Dr. S. Turn onto the signed TRAIL TO S. MCCLELLAN STREET just north of Lake Park. It takes you under the tree canopy of Mount Baker Park.

At this path's end, turn east (left) onto S. McClellan St. It bends south (and becomes Mount Rainier Dr. S.) at a brick storefront building with several snacking/drinking options. Just after that is the ⓫ **Mount Baker Community Club,** a bright and airy meeting/event space.

Backtrack north and then west on McClellan, then immediately turn south (left) onto S. Mount Baker Blvd. One of the Olmsted brothers' park boulevard streets, it meanders for 0.25 mile to the white, neoclassical edifice of Franklin High School (built 1912). Among its famous grads: cartoonist Lynda Barry, actor Keye Luke, choreographer Mark Morris, and musician Kenny G.

Continue along Mount Baker Blvd. to Rainier Ave. and the pedestrian overpass that gets you back to the light-rail station.

This walk intersects with Walk 29 at 18th Ave. S. and the I-90 Trail. It also intersects with Walk 31 at Mount Baker Beach.

Mount Baker

Points of Interest

1 **Mount Baker Station** Rainier Ave S. between S. Winthrop St. and S. Forest St., soundtransit.org

2 **Martin Luther King Jr. Memorial Park** 2200 Martin Luther King Jr. Way S., 206-684-4075, seattle.gov/parks/find/parks/martin-luther-king-jr-memorial-park

3 **FareStart Café** 2100 24th Ave. S., 206-407-2195, farestart.org/cafe-2100

4 **Borracchini's Bakery and Deli** 2307 Rainier Ave. S., 206-325-1550, nowcake.com

5 **Oberto Sausage Factory Store and Deli** 1715 Rainier Ave. S., 206-322-7524, oberto.com/factory-stores

6 **Northwest African American Museum** 2300 S. Massachusetts St., 206-518-6000, naamnw.org

7 **Jimi Hendrix Park** 2400 S. Massachusetts St., 206-684-4075, jimihendrixparkfoundation.org

8 **Our Lady of Mount Virgin Parish** 2800 S. Massachusetts St., 206-324-8521, mountvirgin.org

9 **Bradner Gardens Park** 1730 Bradner Pl. S., 206-684-7481, bradnergardenspark.org

10 **Mount Baker Ridge Viewpoint** 1403 31st Ave. S., 206-684-4075, mtbakerridgeviewpoint.com

11 **Mount Baker Community Club** 2811 Mt. Rainier Dr. S., 206-722-7209, mountbaker.org

30　Beacon Hill
Beckoning

Above: El Centro de la Raza

BOUNDARIES: Beacon Ave. S. at Jefferson Park Golf Course; S. Charles St. and Golf Dr. S.
DISTANCE: 2.75 miles
DIFFICULTY: Easy (almost all flat or downhill)
PARKING: Free parking at Jefferson Park
PUBLIC TRANSIT: Metro route 36; light-rail Beacon Hill Station

Just as there's no capitol on Seattle's Capitol Hill, there's no beacon on Seattle's Beacon Hill. Financier M. Harwood Young simply named it after the famous affluent district in his hometown of Boston.

A few years ago, it was one of the last neighborhoods within Seattle where middle-class and/or immigrant families could afford to buy homes. Now, as gentrification takes over the entire region, organizers are fighting to keep Beacon Hill's diverse character alive.

Walk Description

Start at the ❶ **Jefferson Park Golf Course,** 4101 Beacon Ave. S., built in 1915. Examine the boxy, modern clubhouse and mourn the beautiful old 1930s precursor that was razed, over community preservationists' collective dead bodies, in 2013. The Gillespy Fountain, from the front of the old clubhouse and honoring one of Seattle's early golf promoters, survives.

Take the pedestrian path along the south side of the clubhouse and its adjacent driving range. It curves north then west past a lawn-bowling green in ❷ **Jefferson Park.** Follow the path as it becomes S. Dakota St. Turn north (right) at 16th Ave. S., to the ❸ **Beacon Food Forest,** a big community garden dedicated to growing edible plants and to teaching about how food is grown.

Follow the walking path at the Food Forest's south side back into the main park. This path meanders south of a cricket pitch, then to the north end of the lawn bowling club. It then curves north (left) along the driving range's west side. Take a right when the path forks, at a skateboard park. Keep winding north beyond a community-center building, tennis courts, a fancy family-play area, and two zip lines.

Take a northeasterly (right) fork along the path to the park's northeast edge, at Beacon Ave. S. south of S. Spokane St. Turn north (left) on Beacon.

You're now along the southern end of a street of modest storefronts, classic brick apartments, proud old bungalows, and shade trees. Many of the storefronts now house Asian and Latino restaurants. Particularly enjoy the floral mural outside the former Kucina Filipina at Beacon and S. Hanford St. Another mural, of an Asian girl preparing dinner, adorns the wall of Dragon Auto Repair at Beacon and S. Forest St.

At the northwest corner of Beacon and Forest, the ❹ **Beacon Hill Library** sports a beautiful modern open design with a curved roof and a kinetic boat sculpture on a pole.

Cross Beacon Ave. at the Red Apple supermarket, to the light-rail ❺ **Beacon Hill Station.** The aboveground head house contains the elevators descending 160 feet to the train platforms. Outside are three metal "banners" by artist Carl Smool. A large front plaza at the station blends in with Roberto Maestas Festival St. to the station's north.

Cross Maestas to ❻ **The Station** coffeehouse, a multiethnic community gathering spot. It's on the ground floor of a new affordable-housing complex with an art-festooned plaza, part of ❼ **El Centro de la Raza**'s campus. The original Latino service agency occupies a beautiful old wood-frame elementary school at the campus's north end.

When you're through viewing El Centro, turn east (left) onto Maestas, which retakes the name S. Lander St., downhill to 18th Ave. S. The modern boxy townhome at the southwest corner is NEPO House (*open* spelled backward), the occasional site of arts events. (The rest of the time it's a private home, so don't disturb.)

Turn north (left) down 18th, downhill, around two doglegs. This street is part of the Beacon Hill Greenway, where the city and volunteer groups are making ongoing pedestrian- and bicycle-oriented improvements. You'll see a variety of trees and a variety of home styles: bungalows, brick boxes, postmodern townhomes.

Eighteenth Ave. ends at an entrance to the ❽ **I-90 Trail,** which flows seamlessly into **Daejeon and Sturgus Parks.** Turn left, onto a walking path that winds west and north. Follow the path past a Korean-style pagoda, then past *Equality*, the late Rolon Bert Garner's public artwork of a grid of small concrete Monopoly-style houses in the shadow of one, much larger, house. This work, in turn, is in the shadow of a magnificent view of the downtown skyline.

Eventually you get to the hill's northern tip and its biggest landmark, the 16-story ❾ **Pacific Tower** (originally a Marine hospital, later a U.S. Public Health Service hospital, the Pacific Medical Center, and one of Amazon's former headquarters). Pacific Medical still operates an outpatient clinic on its ground floor.

If you want to continue, cross 12th at the south end of the Jose Rizal Bridge. Keep walking up past Jose Rizal Park along 12th Ave. S. to

The Gillespy Fountain at the Jefferson Park Golf Course clubhouse

❿ **Katie Black's Garden,** a public park that's the last remnant of a once palatial estate built all of cobblestones. Otherwise, remain at the east side of 12th to take a 36 bus back to your start.

This walk ends across the Jose Rizal Bridge from the eastern end of Walk 13. At 18th Ave. S. and the I-90 Trail, it intersects with Walk 29.

Points of Interest

1 **Jefferson Park Golf Course** 4101 Beacon Ave. S., 206-762-4513, premiergc.com
/-jefferson-park-golf-course

2 **Jefferson Park** 3801 Beacon Ave. S., 206-684-4075, seattle.gov/parks/find/parks/jefferson-park

3 **Beacon Food Forest** 15th Ave. S. and S. Dakota St., beaconfoodforest.org

4 **Beacon Hill Library** 2821 Beacon Ave. S., 206-684-4711, spl.org

5 **Beacon Hill Station** Beacon Ave. S. and S. McClellan St., soundtransit.org

6 **The Station** 1600 S. Roberto Maestas Festival St., thestationbh.com

7 **El Centro de la Raza** 2524 16th Ave. S., 206-957-4634, elcentrodelaraza.org

8 **I-90 Trail, Daejeon Park, and Sturgus Park** 904 Sturgus Ave. S., seattle.gov/parks/find/parks
/daejeon-park and seattle.gov/parks/find/parks/sturgus-park

9 **Pacific Tower** 1200 12th Ave. S., pactower.org

10 **Katie Black's Garden** 1150 S. Atlantic St., seattle.gov/parks/find/parks/katie-blacks-garden

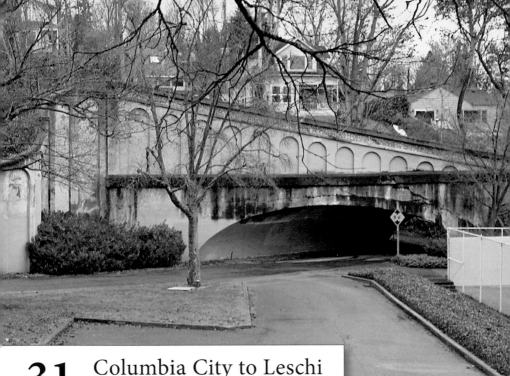

31 Columbia City to Leschi
Quiet Streets and Loud Boats

Above: Former cable-car bridge over Lake Washington Blvd.

BOUNDARIES: Martin Luther King Jr. Way S., S. Hudson St., Lake Washington Blvd., Lakeside Ave. S., and E. Yesler Way
DISTANCE: 5 miles
DIFFICULTY: Moderate (long, with some short uphill segments)
PARKING: Metered street parking at Rainier Ave. S.
PUBLIC TRANSIT: Link light-rail stops at this walk's start; Metro routes 7, 9, 50, and 106 stop near it.

This winding amble through Seattle's southeast corner starts at the former independent town of Columbia City, now a thriving community of classic storefronts and well-preserved middle-class homes. (Some people claim that it is the most diverse neighborhood in the United States.) You continue along the bucolic Lake Washington shoreline, getting a lot closer to the water than you did in Walk 28, then pass another stretch of magnificent water-view estates. Before you return to the lake, you get a glorious glimpse of one of the nation's most spectacular (and lowest) bridges, the modern-day successor to one of the first spans of its type in the world.

Walk Description

Start at the ❶ **Columbia City light-rail station**, Martin Luther King Jr. Way S. and S. Edmunds St. This part of the Central Link route is at ground level. The area surrounding the station is festooned with elaborate public art, including Victoria Fuller's *Global Garden Shovel* (a 35-foot-tall spade bearing relief images of varied flora). Walk southeast on King for two blocks, to S. Hudson St.

Turn left (east) on Hudson and go three blocks, past a small strip mall and modest old homes. The larger house at the northwest corner of 37th Ave. E. and Hudson used to be Columbia City's town hall, when it was a separate town (1892–1907). At the northwest corner of Rainier Ave. S. and Hudson, social service agencies now occupy a 1926 Spanish revival–style police station. Across Rainier, the Tutta Bella artisan-pizza restaurant occupies a classic brick-box storefront.

Turn left (northwest) on the east side of Rainier, through the Columbia City business district. It's a compact string of classic charming buildings. North of Tutta Bella, the ❷ **Columbia City Theater**'s deceptively tiny box-office storefront belies the grand restored concert and performance space behind it. North of it, a handsome Old West wood facade houses the Columbia City Ale House.

Beyond that are three more blocks of handsome and intimate brick, wood, and concrete shop buildings. They contain a bakery, art galleries, hair salons, secondhand shops, clothing boutiques, an old-fashioned meat market, a single-screen cinema, and eateries ranging from BBQ to sushi.

On Rainier's west side north of S. Angeline St., Columbia Park's gently sloping "village green" spans the short distance between the Columbia City branch library (a stunning 1915 Georgian Revival edifice) and the ❸ **Rainier Arts Center** (yet *another* former Christian Science church, now used for performances, classes, and banquets).

Across S. Alaska St., the ❹ **Columbia Funeral Home** occupies a large bungalow behind a well-landscaped front garden. The business has been there since 1917. Before that, it was the childhood home of Leo Lassen, who grew up to be the beloved radio voice of minor league baseball's Seattle Rainiers. The team played a mile north of here, at the now-razed Sick's Stadium.

Continue on Rainier two more blocks, then turn right (east) on S. Genesee St. for eight blocks. Once you pass another pair of strip malls, you're in the sprawling, residential Rainier Valley. It's part of zip code 98118. Columnist Neal Pierce (citing Census Bureau documents) has called this the most ethnically diverse neighborhood in the United States. Whether it's *the* most diverse or

I-90 at the Lake Washington Floating Bridge

not, these blocks definitely mix households of many races, classes, and faiths, within unpretentious homes of many styles.

Beyond 43rd Ave. S., Genesee St. intersects Genesee Park. Turn left (north) and head through this green, mostly flat park to its northern boundary at Lake Washington Blvd. S. Just across the street and along the lakeshore is Stan Sayres Memorial Park, popularly known as The Pits. This series of short piers is home every August to the uniquely Seattle sport of hydroplane boat racing. Any true Seattleite will tell you how the old piston-powered hydros were so much more fun than the turbine-engine boats that race these days. This park's also the site of the ❺ **Mount Baker Rowing and Sailing Center,** where you can learn the art of motorless boating.

Turn left (west) on Lake Washington Blvd., bending northwest then north along the lakeshore. You stay on this street for the rest of this walk. The next mile of it will be along the shore, on a walking and jogging path just east of the vehicular road. As mentioned in Walks 23 and 26, the lake's surface was lowered several feet in the early 20th century. The city held on to this stretch of the new lakefront as a park. You'll see swimmers and sunbathers along this mile on warm days, and joggers by the score every day, along with the big water, the big sky, and the small and big trees. A wall of trees and shrubbery west of the street helps hide civilization's intrusion.

At its northern end, Lake Washington Boulevard Park sports an inland extension known as ❻ **Colman Park**. The street forks here. Take the left fork to continue on Lake Washington Blvd., switchbacking up through Colman Park. You're on a narrow, curving street within a tall tree canopy, offering great contrast between light and shadow. To your right as you leave the park, there's a small brown house. It was one of the last buildings designed by Victor Steinbrueck, the architect and UW professor who led the drive to save the Pike Place Market from redevelopment (Walk 3). Just north of that are some small, rustic cottages designed in 1910–1915 by another prominent local architect, Ellsworth Storey.

Continue north on Lake Washington Blvd. into the Mount Baker neighborhood. The streets here have lake views; the houses are big and fancy. Beyond S. Day St., there's a landscaped clearing where you can see how far from the lake you've come. You're overlooking the twin-span Lake Washington Floating Bridge, the 1989–91 replacement for the original 1940 span, which sank in a windstorm after the new bridge's first span opened. A plaque here honors Lacey V. Murrow, the state transportation chief who supervised the original bridge's creation. (He was the brother of newscaster Edward R. Murrow.) If you descend some steps along the landscaped terrace, you can see the tunnel entrance that greeted travelers on the old bridge with the concrete-relief slogan CITY OF SEATTLE, PORTAL OF THE NORTH PACIFIC. That tunnel, ❼ **I-90 Overpass and Bike Tunnel,** is now for walkers and cyclists only.

Return to Lake Washington Blvd., heading north past posh homes with posher front yards. North of S. Irving St., the road forks again; take the left fork. North of S. Dearborn St., you're back within parkland, specifically the adjoining ❽ **Frink and Leschi Parks**. The street again becomes narrow and curvy, this time heading downhill.

At the fork with S. Jackson St., stay on Lake Washington Blvd. You leave and reenter the park. As you leave the park a second time, you cross under a beautiful concrete underpass (arched on the bottom, angular on top).

You're soon back at the lakeshore at Lakeside Blvd. S., along a small retail strip that includes a deli-mart, a bakery, the ❾ **BluWater Bistro** steak/seafood house, and a commercial marina. To return to your start, take a right on Lakeside to a bus stop for a 27 to downtown. This bus takes a scenic switchback route up Lake Dell Ave. Transfer at Boren Ave. and Yesler Way to a southbound 9 to return to Columbia City, or go downtown and hop on the light-rail.

This walk connects easily to two other walks. It ends 0.75 mile south of Walk 28. At Frink Park you're 0.5 mile east of Walk 12.

Columbia City to Leschi

Points of Interest

1 **Columbia City Station** 4818 Martin Luther King Jr. Way S., soundtransit.org

2 **Columbia City Theater** 4916 Rainier Ave. S., 206-722-3009, columbiacitytheater.com

3 **Rainier Arts Center** 3515 S. Alaska St., 206-725-7517, rainierartscenter.org

4 **Columbia Funeral Home** 4567 Rainier Ave. S., 206-722-1100, columbiafuneralhome.com

5 **Mount Baker Rowing and Sailing Center** 3800 Lake Washington Blvd. S., 206-386-1913, mbrsc.org

6 **Colman Park** 1800 Lake Washington Blvd. S., seattle.gov/parks/find/parks/colman-park

7 **I-90 Overpass and Bike Tunnel** Lake Washington Blvd. S. at S. Day St., traillink.com/trail
/the-i-90-trail.aspx

8 **Frink and Leschi Parks** 398 Lake Washington Blvd. S., seattle.gov/parks/find/parks/frink-park
and seattle.gov/parks/find/parks/leschi-lake-dell-natural-area

9 **BluWater Bistro** 102 Lakeside Ave., 206-328-2233, bluwaterbistro.com

32 Rainier Beach and Kubota Garden
Bamboo and Beauty

Above: *Man-made waterfall within Kubota Garden*

BOUNDARIES: Martin Luther King Jr. Way S., S. Henderson St., Seward Park Ave. S., and S. Norfolk St.
DISTANCE: 3.5 miles
DIFFICULTY: Moderate (1 uphill segment at the start)
PARKING: Free parking at Kubota Garden and at the Atlantic City Boat Ramp
PUBLIC TRANSIT: Link light-rail and Metro routes 36, 50, and 106 stop at this walk's start.

One man's monument to the nurturing power of nature lies at the city's southeast corner. The Kubota Garden was part lifetime hobby, part professional showcase for its landscaper-builder. Now everyone's free to enjoy its 20 acres of hills, valleys, streams, ponds, and garden spaces designed with Japanese techniques and Northwest native plants. You'll get there via a walking path that's a little slice of electrified open space. This walk's back end returns you to the shores of Lake Washington, at a little jewel of a shoreline park.

Walk Description

Start at the light-rail ❶ **Rainier Beach Station,** at Martin Luther King Jr. Way S. and S. Henderson St. As with all the stations on the Central Link line, it's decorated with big, whimsical public art. The dominant piece here is Buster Simpson's *Parable,* a bowl of giant peaches cast in rusted iron, with old rail ties as stems. Across MLK Way there's a building shaped like a Hawaiian longhouse. It's the ❷ **Vegetable Bin Polynesian Deli,** selling both authentic island fare and convenience-store items.

Walk east on Henderson for one block. Take a right turn onto the Chief Sealth Trail. It's a paved walking and biking path along a long, grassy open space, under the transmission towers of municipally owned Seattle City Light.. Since the city already had the land, turning it into a scenic walk was cheap. (The path's asphalt was reclaimed from the light-rail line, which took out a couple of lanes of street.) The whole trail runs 3.5 miles; you wind southeast and a bit uphill on it for 0.5 mile.

For a less scenic but flatter alternate route, continue east on Henderson beyond the intersection with the trail, then turn southeast onto Renton Ave. S.

This segment of the trail empties into Marcus Ave. S., which takes a left turn into S. Roxbury St. Continue on the quiet, residential Roxbury to Renton Ave. S. Turn right onto Renton. Make another right at 55th Ave. S., which leads immediately to the entrance to ❸ **Kubota Garden.**

Now a free city park, Kubota Garden was originally the private hobby and demonstration site for professional gardener Fujitaro Kubota (1879–1973). He and his family spent five decades developing the site, interrupted by the Japanese American internment during World War II. A portion of it is in the formal Japanese garden tradition. The rest was developed according to Kubota's own conception, drawing on an East-meets-West aesthetic. You can follow the map posted just inside the entrance, simply wander, or take a clockwise loop through the grounds' various sections (terrace, waterfall, mountainside, stroll garden, Japanese garden, and stone garden), returning to the entrance.

Back at the garden gate, take a left onto 55th, then take another left to backtrack on Renton Ave. for one block.

Turn right (north) on 54th Ave. S., making a right-left dogleg at S. Roxbury St. These are low-density blocks of homes that get fancier the closer they are to Lake Washington. Continue on 54th to Rainier Ave. S. Turn right (east) on Rainier and travel one long block to Seward Park Ave. S., past affordable food spots of both indie and franchise varieties.

If you want to lengthen your walk, continue on Rainier 0.25 mile to the Stone House Café and Bakery. Its two stone-clad buildings were built in the 1920s, originally as a gas station/garage. Then backtrack.

Side Trip: Seward Park

To make this walk longer, continue north on Seward Park Ave. S. beyond S. Henderson St. After 1.75 miles, turn east on S. Juneau St. and into Seward Park. The 300-acre nature park sits on its own peninsula. You can take a 3-mile walk around the lakefront, which includes a swimming beach, and follow inland trails through 120 acres of old-growth forest, teeming with plants and birds. Seward is also directly reachable on a 39 bus. More information is at the Friends of Seward Park website, sewardpark.org.

In either event, now turn left (northwest) onto Seward Park Ave. S. To your right, you pass a private marina and yacht club. Then you reach the public ❹ **Atlantic City Boat Ramp,** the southernmost of three adjacent city parks. There's some green space and some open shoreline just north of the dock, as the site segues into ❺ **Beer Sheva Park** (renamed after Seattle's Israeli sister city). If you have the time, you can stroll a little farther north into Pritchard Island Beach Park. There's a beach there, but not an island. When the lake was lowered last century, a shallow slough between the mainland and a small private island became aboveground wetlands. Most of the Pritchard park is on this strip. The park also has a beach and a rental meeting hall.

When you have finished visiting these parks, return to the intersection of Seward Park and Henderson, just north of the boat dock. Turn left (west) on Henderson. To your right are Rainier Beach High School and the K–8 South Shore School. The latter includes Rainier Henderson Plaza, a handsome public square featuring a circular labyrinth path. (It's similar to the labyrinth at St. Paul's Episcopal Church in lower Queen Anne, Walk 18.) Free afternoon concerts are held here in the summer. The plaza adjoins the ❻ **Rainier Beach Community Center,** a large rental space for events of all types.

Continue west on Henderson, back to the Rainier Beach Station.

This walk starts 2.5 miles south of Walk 31's start.

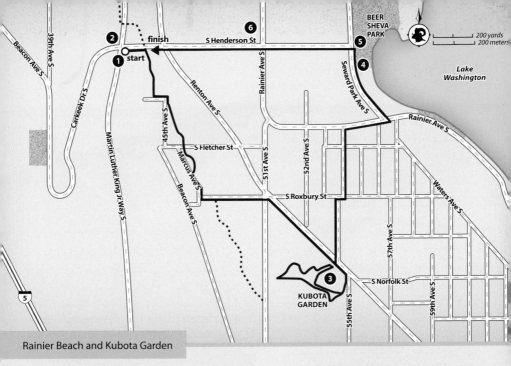

Rainier Beach and Kubota Garden

Points of Interest

1. **Rainier Beach Station** 9132 Martin Luther King Jr. Way S., soundtransit.org

2. **Vegetable Bin Polynesian Deli** 8825 Martin Luther King Jr. Way S., 206-725-0543

3. **Kubota Garden** 9817 55th Ave. S., 206-725-5060, kubotagarden.org

4. **Atlantic City Boat Ramp** 8702 Seward Park Ave. S., 206-684-7249, seattle.gov/parks/find/parks
   /atlantic-city-boat-ramp

5. **Beer Sheva Park** 8650 55th Ave. S., seattle.gov/parks/find/parks/beer-sheva-park

6. **Rainier Beach Community Center** 8825 Rainier Ave. S., 206-386-1925, seattle.gov
   /parks/centers/rainierbeach.htm

33 Georgetown
Art Meets Industry

BOUNDARIES: 1st Ave. S., Airport Way S., S. Lucile St., and 13th Ave. S.
DISTANCE: 2.5 miles
DIFFICULTY: Easy (all flat)
PARKING: Free street parking along S. Orcas St.
PUBLIC TRANSIT: Metro routes 131 and 132 stop near this route's start.

Georgetown, another of the former independent towns annexed into Seattle, is an urban island surrounded by industry, a freeway, two freight yards, and a cargo airport. In recent years, it has gone from neglected hamlet to arts mecca. This is partly because those decades of neglect had left a main street of rugged brick and metal-clad postfrontier storefronts, across from the 0.25-mile long edifice of a pre-Prohibition brewing plant. These spaces nurtured what *Seattle Weekly* writer Laura Cassidy called a style of "post-squat, industrial bohemian chic." Georgetown's residential streets have their own charm, with many ornate Victorian and Edwardian home styles you won't find in most of Seattle. You'll also see a genuine piece of reclaimed 1950s roadside kitsch, plus a couple of new hangouts styled as homages to roadside kitsch.

Walk Description

Start on the east side of 1st Ave. S., walking north from S. Orcas St. You soon spot the retro-roadhouse facade of ❶ **Slim's Last Chance Chili Shack**. The kitsch-nostalgia diner, saloon, and music spot is just as whimsical inside. A similar vibe carries on next door at Iron Pig BBQ.

Turn right (east) on S. Lucile St. at the fab '50s neon of La Hacienda Motel, one of many that once flourished along and near US 99 in the pre-interstate era. Approaching 4th Ave. S., you pass a garden statuary lot (always fun to look at). Across 4th, the Vac Shop displays a variety of classic vacuums out front, along with at least one '50s sci-fi robot and a sign promoting free bibles inside.

Turn right (south) on 4th and travel two blocks. At 4th and Orcas, the Marco Polo is a comfy neighborhood sports bar with exceptional fried chicken.

Turn left back onto Orcas, heading east. To your left, the Blu Grouse is a cute little bungalow turned into a restaurant/bar. The much, much bigger building to your right is the ❷ **Seattle Design Center,** filled with home-furnishings showrooms. Originally open only to interior designers and contractors, it's now open to the public for browsing and occasional sample sales.

Turn left (north) on 6th Ave. S. and continue two blocks back to Lucile. Turn right and walk east for four blocks on Lucile, past loading docks and low-rise offices, toward Airport Way S., Georgetown's main drag.

Turn right (southeast) onto the right side of Airport Way. It runs for nearly 0.5 mile of recent, older, and really old low-rise storefronts and ex-hotels. Some look like Old West movie sets. Some look like standard neighborhood retail buildings. Some are more (and more authentically) restored than others. All this variety simply adds to the strip's funky charm. The first arty joints you see are Kirk Albert Vintage Furnishings and Georgetown Liquor Co. (a bar and veggie restaurant). A little farther down, Stellar Pizza serves up cool mod design and vintage pinball games along with its food and drinks. Just west of Airport on Corson Ave. S., the Corson Building is an intimate ultrafoodie restaurant, serving local organic ingredients in a 1910 Spanish-eclectic building behind a rose-covered iron fence.

Cross Corson, under a freeway on-ramp, to continue down Airport Way. To your left, you soon see the sprawling brick edifices of Rainier Brewing's pre-Prohibition plant. It houses several art studios, open on second Saturday art walks. (Rainier's post-Prohibition production was at an equally historic site, 2 miles north of here.) To your right, the funky, artsy storefronts continue with the Georgetown Ballroom, the old-timey Jules Maes bar, Full Throttle Bottles (a beer-wine store with a music and meeting space in back), and the ❸ **Georgetown Trailer Park Mall** (art, antiques, and vintage clothes sold in vintage camping trailers).

South of S. Vale St., just beyond the Big Peoples Scooter lot (headquarters of the Vespa revival), the Horton Building is ground zero of the Georgetown arts scene. In this full-block former hotel are ❹ **Georgetown Records** (vintage vinyl kings), **Fantagraphics Bookstore and Gallery** (a retail outlet for the leading graphic novel publishers in the United States), the 9 Lb. Hammer bar, the Square Knot diner, the All City Coffee espresso joint, a recording studio, and artist live-and-work spaces. On the southern wall is artist Kathryn Rathke's neon sign depicting Georgetown landmarks beneath the face of a lady shushing at a loud airplane approaching Boeing Field.

Turn right (south) on 13th Ave. S. To your right, the Miller Building, a 1929 brick storefront block, still looks gorgeous despite the loss of the venerable Georgetown Pharmacy and its classic '40s neon sign. To your left on the next block, the old Georgetown City Hall is a handsome two-story red-and-white structure with a small clock tower on top. It was built in 1909, just a year before Seattle took over the previously independent town.

Turn right (southwest) on S. Albro Pl. To your left in the distance, a big checkerboard wall marks the visual approach for aircraft landing at King County Airport-Boeing Field. The region's first major airfield, it's now used mostly for cargo, charters, and general aviation.

The restored Hat 'n' Boots *at Oxbow Park*

Turn right (west) on S. Eddy St. Continue two blocks, then turn left (south) on Carleton Ave. S. To your right halfway down the block, a former vacant lot is now ❺ **Oxbow Park**. The pocket park is named for a bend in the Duwamish River, which was taken out when the river was redredged to be more barge friendly. The park is home to the *Hat 'n' Boots*. This giant cowboy hat, man's boot, and woman's boot were originally the office and restrooms of a '50s gas station on nearby East Marginal Way S. The city moved the roadside attractions, which volunteers then restored.

Across Carleton, the turreted Victorian ❻ **Georgetown Castle** is the location of frequent

Side Trip: Museum of Flight

Situated at Boeing Field's southwest end, the Museum of Flight celebrates Seattle's heritage as the world capital of commercial aircraft and a major center for aviation in general. It incorporates William Boeing's original Red Barn factory, plus permanent and rotating displays covering a century of human flight. The museum's own collection includes more than 150 historic aircraft, spacecraft, and associated artifacts.

alleged ghost sightings. The Travel Channel called it one of the most terrifying places in America. You can see it on guided tours every Halloween season.

Turn left (east) on S. Warsaw St. At the northwest corner of Warsaw and Ellis Ave. S., **❼ Mini Mart City Park** is a 1930s gas station that conceptual artists John Sutton, Ben Beres, and Zac Culler have taken over. They plan to turn it into a landscaped public green space, once the soil has been decontaminated or replaced.

Continue one more block on Warsaw toward the **❽ Georgetown Steam Plant,** a 1906 oil- and coal-powered electricity generating station. Most of its equipment is still installed, and a volunteer group, the Georgetown PowerPlant Museum, keeps it in good shape. The building also hosts a model-train club, the Puget Sound Garden Railway Society. The two groups hold open houses the second Saturday of each month. Most of the rest of the time, you have to view the handsome structure (one of the first reinforced-concrete buildings on the Pacific Coast) from behind a fence.

Return to Warsaw and Ellis. Turn left (south) on Ellis. To your right, you see working-class homes in various degrees of fanciness and upkeep. To your left, warehouses and truck lots. Behind that, the west side of Boeing Field.

Head right (west) on S. Myrtle St. Go a little more than one block, then turn right (northwest) on the right side of East Marginal for two more blocks. You pass the Airlane, an old flophouse-style hotel still in use, and the forlorn sign of the closed Chief Seattle Motel. The **❾ Connections Museum Seattle,** a volunteer-curated collection of analog-era telephone gear, is in an old Bell System switching center at East Marginal and Corson Ave. S. It's open only on Sundays.

From here you can take a 124 bus back to 4th and Orcas. Or you can walk 2 miles southeast on East Marginal, or take a southbound 124, to the Museum of Flight at Boeing Field's southern end.

This walk starts 1.25 miles south of Walk 14.

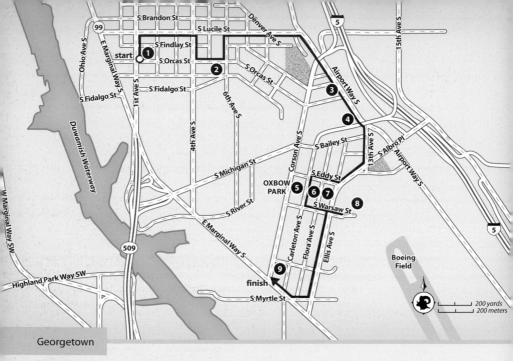

Points of Interest

1. **Slim's Last Chance Chili Shack** 5506 1st Ave. S., 206-762-7900, slimslastchance.com

2. **Seattle Design Center** 5701 6th Ave. S., 800-762-1200, seattledesigncenter.com

3. **Georgetown Trailer Park Mall** 5805 Airport Way S., georgetowntrailerpark.com

4. **Georgetown Records and Fantagraphics Bookstore and Gallery** 1201 S. Vale St., 206-762-5638, georgetownrecords.net and fantagraphics.com

5. **Oxbow Park** 6430 Corson Ave. S., seattle.gov/parks/find/parks/oxbow-park

6. **Georgetown Castle** 6420 Carleton Ave. S.

7. **Mini Mart City Park** 6525 Ellis Ave. S., minimartcitypark.com

8. **Georgetown Steam Plant** 6605 13th Ave. S., 206-763-2542, georgetownsteamplant.org

9. **Connections Museum Seattle** 7000 East Marginal Way S., 206-767-3012, museumofcommunications.org

34 West Marginal Way
Heading to "Port"

Above: *West Duwamish Greenbelt*

BOUNDARIES: 16th Ave. SW, SW Holden St., W. Marginal Way SW, and SW Chelan St.
DISTANCE: 4 miles
DIFFICULTY: Moderate (almost all flat or downhill)
PARKING: Free street parking
PUBLIC TRANSIT: Metro routes 125 and 128 stop near this route's start. Routes 21, 50, 120, and 125 stop at or near its end.

"The Real West Marginal Way," to quote the title of the late local poet Richard Hugo's autobiography, is a place where shipping and heavy industry exist side by side with pieces of restored natural settings along the Duwamish River. The river itself, the original birthplace of Boeing airplanes and Kenworth trucks, was redredged and rerouted decades ago to provide a deeper and straighter passage for ocean-bound freighters. In recent years, a walking and biking path has been added along West Marginal, along with a series of small parks that re-create pieces of the original Duwamish environment. Your walk starts with a downhill hike through a greenbelt, one of Seattle's stretches of protected woodlands.

Walk Description

Start on SW Holden St., walking east from 16th Ave. SW in West Seattle's residential heartland.

After one block, Holden curves northeast, then southeast. The most striking building along this stretch is the ❶ **Paradise of Praise Church**. It's an asymmetrical, wood-frame storefront church that looks older than it is (built only in 1995). Otherwise, this six-block segment mostly has modest homes and simple 1960s-era apartments, interspersed after 12th Ave. SW with rows of townhomes built in the late 1990s and early 2000s.

Turn left (north) on the right side of Highland Park Way SW. This street bends east and downhill through the ❷ **West Duwamish Greenbelt,** a huge canopy of second-growth forest along the West Seattle peninsula's eastern bluff, preserved partly to help prevent erosion. You'll think you're on a gently curving country road, at least until the semis careen by. Fortunately, you have a separate walking and biking lane to the east of the road. To your left approaching the bottom of the hill, a sign invites you onto a network of trails through the greenbelt.

This rural vibe ends promptly once you reach the bottom of the hill. The Duwamish River's working waterfront comes into view, along with West Marginal Way SW. Cross at the light to the northeast corner of this intersection.

From there head left (north) on the Duwamish Bikeway paralleling West Marginal's east side. To your left, the Duwamish Greenbelt continues, occasionally interrupted by warehouses and metalwork plants. (This part of the greenbelt has especially scenic fall foliage.) To your right, you see ❸ **Portside Coffee,** an espresso stand shaped like the bow of a steel merchant ship.

North of Portside is a huge freight yard, with cargo containers stacked up like huge LEGO constructions. North of that are cement and asphalt plants that were quite busy during the construction boom years but are slightly less so nowadays. They're still magnificent structures, highlighted by big gray cylindrical towers huddled together in clumps.

Just north of these plants, the bikeway takes a dogleg detour away from West Marginal and toward ❹ **Terminal 107 Park**. It's one of several waterfront park spaces recently added along the Duwamish. The Port of Seattle built them under a city law requiring the port to add public space whenever it remodels a shipping facility. This one has nearly 0.5 mile of public shoreline, put back into a more-or-less natural state with the help of the nonprofit People for Puget Sound.

It has views of Kellogg Island, a tiny islet that's also been deindustrialized. It has eagles, ospreys, and migrating salmon. (Signs warn against eating fish caught here.)

Continue north as the port-owned park Terminal 107 Park segues seamlessly into the city-owned Herring's House Park. The name is a translation of the original Duwamish tribal name for this spot. Archaeologists believe that humans have inhabited the area around this riverbank for more than 1,400 years. The city's section of the park includes a natural intertidal basin at the shoreline, along with areas of marsh, meadow, forest, and a narrow beach. It also features a five-eighths-scale model of a 1920s fishing boat. Its creator, artist Donald Fels, modeled it after boats that were made at shops that once stood at this site.

Return from the park to the bikeway, walking north. To the left will be the ❺ **Duwamish Longhouse and Cultural Center**. The Duwamish tribal headquarters is the first new tribal longhouse built in Seattle in more than 140 years. It's home to art exhibits, performances, and community events.

A still-active cement plant

Side Trip: South Seattle College

South Seattle College's north side has a fastidiously landscaped 6-acre arboretum. Created in 1978, it serves both as an elegant walking and picnicking spot and as a living laboratory for the school's landscape-horticulture program. It also includes a student-run garden store.

Next to the arboretum is the Seattle Chinese Garden. This 4.5-acre hilltop site offers a magnificent outdoor pavilion and tremendous views of the Duwamish Greenbelt bluff and the Duwamish Waterway. The college itself has a renowned culinary arts department. It operates three on-campus restaurants (from cafeteria style to formal dining) and a pastry shop.

The bikeway ends just beyond here. Cross to West Marginal's left (west) side, the only side where there's now a sidewalk. The street bends northwest here, past warehouses, bus lots, and a kitchen-supply showroom.

Just north of the intersection of West Marginal and SW Dakota St., there's a narrow paved pathway behind an open gate to your right. It's the road to ❻ **Terminal 105 Park**, another Port of Seattle public space project. Along with 220 feet of restored shoreline, it has a fishing pier, a launch for nonmotorized boats, a restored mudflat for fish to feed, public restrooms, and a picnic area with great views of the river and Mount Rainier.

Continue walking northwest. To your right there's another big cement plant and a diving and salvage company. To your left, a narrow, two-story, brick-front office building with arched windows is an island of dignified vintage architecture in these more rough-hewn environs. Behind it are 16th and 17th Aves., short residential streets with pre-1940 rooming and shotgun houses.

Just before you walk beneath the tall West Seattle Bridge, the old Riverside Mill now houses a motor-freight yard; a sign commemorates the property's lumber-making past. Continue on West Marginal as it bends west, becoming Chelan Ave. SW at the ❼ **Chelan Cafe** (Walk 14).

To get back to your start, cross to Chelan and SW Spokane St. and catch a 125 bus. If you have the time and energy, consider a stopover along the 125 route at ❽ **South Seattle College** (see sidebar, above).

This walk connects easily to two other walks. It ends at the same place as Walk 22. At West Marginal and Highland Park Way you're 1.25 miles from Walk 35, across the 1st Ave. S. bridge.

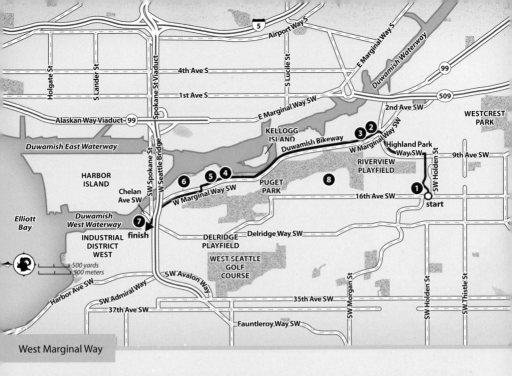

West Marginal Way

Points of Interest

① **Paradise of Praise Church** 1316 SW Holden St., 206-764-1053, paradiseofpraise.org

② **West Duwamish Greenbelt and Puget Park** Highland Park Way SW and West Marginal Way SW, seattle.gov/parks/find/parks/west-duwamish-greenbelt and seattle.gov/parks/find/parks/puget-park

③ **Portside Coffee** 6720 West Marginal Way SW, 206-762-7509

④ **Terminal 107 Park** 4700 West Marginal Way SW, portseattle.org

⑤ **Duwamish Longhouse and Cultural Center** 4705 West Marginal Way SW, 206-431-1582, duwamishtribe.org

⑥ **Terminal 105 Park** 4260 West Marginal Way SW, portseattle.org

⑦ **Chelan Cafe** 3527 Chelan Ave. SW, 206-932-7383

⑧ **South Seattle College** 6000 16th Ave. SW, 206-764-5300, southseattle.edu

35   West Seattle: The Junction to Admiral
A Whole Other City

BOUNDARIES: SW Edmunds St., 42nd Ave. SW, SW Admiral Way, and SW Stevens St.
DISTANCE: 3.5 miles
DIFFICULTY: Moderate (2 brief uphill segments toward the end)
PARKING: Free street parking and pay lots
PUBLIC TRANSIT: Metro routes 22, 37, 50, 54, 55, 57, 128 and RapidRide C stop near this route's start.
    Routes 50, 55, and 128 stop near its end.

West Seattle lies on a separate peninsula from the rest of the city, and it sometimes seems like a separate world. Our last four walks traverse different parts of it, beginning with its commercial and transit hub. The Junction was named after the streetcar lines that intersected it, creating the obvious site for West Seattle's business district. Like many of the neighborhood retail strips you've seen in this book, it's now abloom with cool independent stores, galleries, restaurants, and bars.

Your trek continues past a classic high school building and a nautical-themed movie theater. It ends at one of the city's last patches of never-logged forestland.

Walk Description

Start on California Ave. SW, walking north from SW Edmunds St. This is the start of the Junction, West Seattle's principal shopping district. This first long block comprises some standard American one- and two-story main-street storefronts. Many offer traditional main-street wares—furniture, bedding, pet supplies, prescriptions. Others are a little more uncommon, such as Bakery Nouveau (butter croissants to die for), ❶ **Husky Deli** (home-style ice cream to kill for), and ❷ **ArtsWest** (a theater and art gallery).

The next intersection is California and SW Alaska St. The Junction got its name from the streetcar lines that used to cross here. It's still a major bus transfer point. To your left just beyond Alaska, ❸ **Easy Street Records and Cafe** is a full-service music outlet plus a full-service diner. As one of the store's ad slogans explains: "Because downloads don't come with fries." Next door on Alaska, the ❹ **Virago Gallery** sells art, jewelry, and gifts "by women artists and their allies."

As you resume your northbound trek on California, you pass three more long blocks of storefronts. They include antiques shops, a yoga studio, used-book stores, jewelers, coffee-houses, teahouses, snack shops, and lounge restaurants. Two favorites among the latter include the funky-but-chic West 5 and the exquisitely posh Jak's Grill. There are also handsome low-rise churches, The Junction Church and First Lutheran.

To your left just north of SW Dakota St., the former California Avenue Substation is a 1930s neoclassical brick box with terra-cotta ornamentation. It's also a remnant of the era (1901–1951) when Seattle had two competing electric companies, the city-owned City Light and the private Seattle Electric (later renamed Puget Power, still operating in the suburbs as Puget Sound Energy). North of that, and for the next several blocks, California becomes a quiet tree-lined arterial, mostly occupied by mid-century homes and apartments.

To your left near California and SW Hinds St., a German-style pub and an indie pizza place mark the start of the Admiral district. To your right a little farther north lie West Seattle High School and the adjacent Hiawatha Playfield. The school's original facade, built in 1917, bears a number of ancient symbols of varying origins, from pentacles and Greek crosses to ram's-head gargoyles.

Wiseman's Appliance and TV, a throwback to the days of small neighborhood appliance stores (only with all new merchandise), stands just south of California and SW Admiral Way, the Admiral district's main intersection. Just north of it, on your left, the nautical-themed ❺ **Admiral**

Theatre still bears much of its 1940s Art Moderne charm, despite an unfortunate 1973 "upgrade" that removed or covered up a lot of its cool decor (it's been re-remodeled since). Three blocks farther north, as the street segues back into residential use, ❻ **Admiral Congregational United Church of Christ** is an angular, monochromatic monument of early 1960s modernism tucked behind a pocket park.

Turn right (northeast) on Ferry Ave. SW for one block, then immediately turn right (south) on 42nd Ave. SW for four blocks. This stretch starts in a quiet residential zone with big trees and shrubbery and transitions at the West Seattle Public Library on SW College St. This elegant brick structure was built in 1910 with an Andrew Carnegie grant. Just south of it is a Metropolitan Market upscale grocery, across from a condo and retail behemoth.

Turn right (west) on SW Admiral Way, back toward the intersection with California. To your right, just beyond the Parliament Tavern is the ❼ **Vidiot** arcade and bar. From 1950 to 2002 it was the Admiral Benbow Inn, a legendary comfort-food eatery and hangout bar. Its barroom has a Spanish-galleon theme, with fake sunlight streaming through stained glass aft windows. Just across Admiral is the ❽ **Admiral Bird** and **Flower Lab**, a combo bar and florist shop.

Continue on Admiral. It becomes a wide residential arterial, wending southwest and down-hill, then west again. In the distance you can get a peek of the waters off Alki Point (Walk 15).

Turn left (south) onto 53rd Ave. SW, initially a bit uphill. Your perseverance with this late incline will prove worth it once 53rd bends west into SW Stevens St., offering a magnificent view of Puget Sound and (on a good day) the Olympic Mountains.

Just before Stevens reunites with Admiral, you're at the north entrance to ❾ **Schmitz Preserve Park**. These 53 acres comprise some of the last old-growth woods left within the Seattle city limits. This land has been pretty much left in the state it was in when it was donated to the city, in tracts between 1908 and 1912. What work has been done on it has been to restore more of its original appearance, by taking out an interior parking lot and "daylighting" a creek that had been hidden in underground drainpipes.

From here you can wander through Schmitz or return to Admiral Way and get a 50 bus back to the Junction.

At Ferry Ave. SW you're 0.5 mile southwest of Walk 15.

West Seattle: The Junction to Admiral

Points of Interest

1 **Husky Deli** 4721 California Ave. SW, 206-937-2810, huskydeli.com

2 **ArtsWest** 4711 California Ave. SW, 206-938-0963, artswest.org

3 **Easy Street Records and Cafe** 4559 California Ave. SW, 206-938-3279, easystreetonline.com

4 **Virago Gallery** 4306 SW Alaska St., 206-933-2444, viragogallery.com

5 **Admiral Theatre** 2343 California Ave. SW, 206-938-0360, farawayentertainment.com/location /admiral-theater

6 **Admiral Congregational United Church of Christ** 4320 SW Hill St., 206-932-2928, admiralchurch.org

7 **Vidiot** 4210 SW Admiral Way, vidiotarcadebar.com

8 **Admiral Bird** 2600 California Ave. SW, 206-305-7182, thirstiestbirds.com
Flower Lab 206-935-2587, seattleflowerlab.com

9 **Schmitz Preserve Park** 5551 SW Admiral Way, seattle.gov/parks/find/parks/schmitz-preserve-park

Appendix A: Walks by Theme

The following walks have at least one major component that fits the theme.

Architecture

Pioneer Square (Walk 1)
Downtown: Off the Grid (Walk 2)
Pike Place Market, 1st Ave., and the Waterfront (Walk 3)
Downtown: The Retail Core and Financial District (Walk 4)
Pike–Pine (Walk 5)
First Hill (Walk 6)
Belltown and Seattle Center (Walk 7)
South Lake Union (Walk 8)
Fairview and Eastlake (Walk 9)
West Capitol Hill and Broadway (Walk 10)
East Capitol Hill (Walk 11)
Chinatown-International District (Walk 13)
SoDo Industrial District (Walk 14)
Discovery Park to Ballard Locks (Walk 16)
Wallingford to Roosevelt (Walk 21)
The U District and University of Washington Campus (Walk 25)
Mount Baker (Walk 29)
Beacon Hill (Walk 30)
Georgetown (Walk 33)
West Seattle: The Junction to Admiral (Walk 35)

The Arts

Pioneer Square (Walk 1)
Downtown: Off the Grid (Walk 2)
Pike Place Market, 1st Ave., and the Waterfront (Walk 3)
Downtown: The Retail Core and Financial District (Walk 4)
Pike–Pine (Walk 5)
First Hill (Walk 6)
Belltown and Seattle Center (Walk 7)
South Lake Union (Walk 8)
West Capitol Hill and Broadway (Walk 10)
East Capitol Hill (Walk 11)
Central District (Walk 12)
Chinatown-International District (Walk 13)
Fremont (Walk 19)
Phinney Ridge and Greenwood (Walk 20)
Wallingford to Roosevelt (Walk 21)

Ballard (Walk 22)
Ravenna and Laurelhurst (Walk 24)
The U District and University of Washington Campus (Walk 25)
Columbia City to Leschi (Walk 31)
Georgetown (Walk 33)
West Seattle: The Junction to Admiral (Walk 35)

Classic Seattle Neighborhoods

Pioneer Square (Walk 1)
Pike Place Market, 1st Ave., and the Waterfront (Walk 3)
Pike–Pine (Walk 5)
First Hill (Walk 6)
Belltown and Seattle Center (Walk 7)
South Lake Union (Walk 8)
Fairview and Eastlake (Walk 9)
West Capitol Hill and Broadway (Walk 10)
East Capitol Hill (Walk 11)
Central District (Walk 12)
Chinatown-International District (Walk 13)
Alki (Walk 15)
Magnolia (Walk 17)
Queen Anne Hill (Walk 18)
Fremont (Walk 19)
Phinney Ridge and Greenwood (Walk 20)
Wallingford to Roosevelt (Walk 21)
Ballard (Walk 22)
Green Lake (Walk 23)
The U District and University of Washington Campus (Walk 25)
Madrona and Madison Park (Walk 28)
Mount Baker (Walk 29)
Beacon Hill (Walk 30)
Columbia City to Leschi (Walk 31)
Georgetown (Walk 33)
West Seattle: The Junction to Admiral (Walk 35)

Dining and Entertainment

Pioneer Square (Walk 1)
Pike Place Market, 1st Ave., and the Waterfront (Walk 3)
Downtown: The Retail Core and Financial District (Walk 4)
Pike–Pine (Walk 5)
First Hill (Walk 6)
Belltown and Seattle Center (Walk 7)
South Lake Union (Walk 8)

Dining and Entertainment *(continued)*

West Capitol Hill and Broadway (Walk 10)
East Capitol Hill (Walk 11)
Central District (Walk 12)
Chinatown-International District (Walk 13)
SoDo Industrial District (Walk 14)
Alki (Walk 15)
Discovery Park to Ballard Locks (Walk 16)
Magnolia (Walk 17)
Queen Anne Hill (Walk 18)
Fremont (Walk 19)
Phinney Ridge and Greenwood (Walk 20)
Wallingford to Roosevelt (Walk 21)
Ballard (Walk 22)
Green Lake (Walk 23)
Ravenna and Laurelhurst (Walk 24)
The U District and University of Washington Campus (Walk 25)
Madrona and Madison Park (Walk 28)
Mount Baker (Walk 29)
Columbia City to Leschi (Walk 31)
Georgetown (Walk 33)
West Seattle: The Junction to Admiral (Walk 35)

History

Pioneer Square (Walk 1)
Pike Place Market, 1st Ave., and the Waterfront (Walk 3)
Downtown: The Retail Core and Financial District (Walk 4)
Pike–Pine (Walk 5)
First Hill (Walk 6)
Belltown and Seattle Center (Walk 7)
South Lake Union (Walk 8)
West Capitol Hill and Broadway (Walk 10)
East Capitol Hill (Walk 11)
Central District (Walk 12)
Chinatown-International District (Walk 13)
SoDo Industrial District (Walk 14)
Alki (Walk 15)
Discovery Park to Ballard Locks (Walk 16)
Fremont (Walk 19)
Wallingford to Roosevelt (Walk 21)
Ballard (Walk 22)
The U District and University of Washington Campus (Walk 25)

Foster Island and the Arboretum (Walk 26)
Mount Baker (Walk 29)
Beacon Hill (Walk 30)
Columbia City to Leschi (Walk 31)
Georgetown (Walk 33)
West Marginal Way (Walk 34)

Industry

Pike Place Market, 1st Ave., and the Waterfront (Walk 3)
Pike–Pine (Walk 5)
Fairview and Eastlake (Walk 9)
Chinatown-International District (Walk 13)
SoDo Industrial District (Walk 14)
Discovery Park to Ballard Locks (Walk 16)
Fremont (Walk 19)
Ballard (Walk 22)
Georgetown (Walk 33)
West Marginal Way (Walk 34)

The Music Scene

Pioneer Square (Walk 1)
Pike–Pine (Walk 5)
Belltown and Seattle Center (Walk 7)
South Lake Union (Walk 8)
West Capitol Hill and Broadway (Walk 10)
Chinatown-International District (Walk 13)
SoDo Industrial District (Walk 14)
Fremont (Walk 19)
Wallingford to Roosevelt (Walk 21)
Ballard (Walk 22)
Ravenna and Laurelhurst (Walk 24)
The U District and University of Washington Campus (Walk 25)
Georgetown (Walk 33)
West Seattle: The Junction to Admiral (Walk 35)

Parks

Pioneer Square (Walk 1)
Downtown: Off the Grid (Walk 2)
Pike Place Market, 1st Ave., and the Waterfront (Walk 3)
Belltown and Seattle Center (Walk 7)
South Lake Union (Walk 8)

Parks *(continued)*

East Capitol Hill (Walk 11)
Alki (Walk 15)
Discovery Park to Ballard Locks (Walk 16)
Magnolia (Walk 17)
Queen Anne Hill (Walk 18)
Fremont (Walk 19)
Phinney Ridge and Greenwood (Walk 20)
Wallingford to Roosevelt (Walk 21)
Green Lake (Walk 23)
Ravenna and Laurelhurst (Walk 24)
The U District and University of Washington Campus (Walk 25)
Foster Island and the Arboretum (Walk 26)
Interlaken and Montlake (Walk 27)
Madrona and Madison Park (Walk 28)
Mount Baker (Walk 29)
Beacon Hill (Walk 30)
Columbia City to Leschi (Walk 31)
Rainier Beach and Kubota Garden (Walk 32)
Georgetown (Walk 33)
West Marginal Way (Walk 34)
West Seattle: The Junction to Admiral (Walk 35)

Shopping

Pioneer Square (Walk 1)
Downtown: Off the Grid (Walk 2)
Pike Place Market, 1st Ave., and the Waterfront (Walk 3)
Downtown: The Retail Core and Financial District (Walk 4)
Pike–Pine (Walk 5)
Belltown and Seattle Center (Walk 7)
South Lake Union (Walk 8)
West Capitol Hill and Broadway (Walk 10)
Chinatown-International District (Walk 13)
SoDo Industrial District (Walk 14)
Magnolia (Walk 17)
Queen Anne Hill (Walk 18)
Fremont (Walk 19)
Phinney Ridge and Greenwood (Walk 20)
Wallingford to Roosevelt (Walk 21)
Ballard (Walk 22)
Ravenna and Laurelhurst (Walk 24)
The U District and University of Washington Campus (Walk 25)
Columbia City to Leschi (Walk 31)

Trees

Views

Views *(continued)*

West Marginal Way (Walk 34)
West Seattle: The Junction to Admiral (Walk 35)

Water

Pioneer Square (Walk 1)
Pike Place Market, 1st Ave., and the Waterfront (Walk 3)
South Lake Union (Walk 8)
Fairview and Eastlake (Walk 9)
Alki (Walk 15)
Discovery Park to Ballard Locks (Walk 16)
Magnolia (Walk 17)
Queen Anne Hill (Walk 18)
Fremont (Walk 19)
Ballard (Walk 22)
Green Lake (Walk 23)
The U District and University of Washington Campus (Walk 25)
Foster Island and the Arboretum (Walk 26)
Madrona and Madison Park (Walk 28)
Mount Baker (Walk 29)
Columbia City to Leschi (Walk 31)
Rainier Beach and Kubota Garden (Walk 32)
West Marginal Way (Walk 34)

Appendix B: Further Reading

Books

Becker, Paula, Alan J. Stein, and HistoryLink staff. *The Future Remembered: The 1962 Seattle World's Fair and Its Legacy*. Seattle: Seattle Center Foundation/HistoryLink, 2011. What visionaries thought the 21st century would be (or at least look) like and their permanent Seattle Center legacy.

Crowley, Walt, and HistoryLink staff. *Seattle & King County Timeline*. Seattle: History Ink with University of Washington Press, 2001. A slim volume jam-packed with pictures of and fun facts about the Jet City.

Duncan, Don. *Meet Me at the Center: The Story of Seattle Center from the Beginnings to the 1962 Seattle World's Fair to the 21st Century*. Seattle: Seattle Center Foundation, 1992. The center, the world's fair that spawned it, and how the city has celebrated itself.

Elenga, Maureen R. *Seattle Architecture*. Seattle: Seattle Architecture Foundation, 2007. From Pioneer Square to Seattle Center, downtown Seattle's major structures and how they were designed and built.

Garbacik, Jaimee, ed. *Ghosts of Seattle Past*. Seattle: Chin Music Press, 2017. Essays, interviews, and comics about stuff that's not here anymore.

Johnston, Norman J. *The Fountain and the Mountain: The University of Washington Campus in Seattle*. Seattle: Documentary Media, 2003. Gorgeous coffee-table tribute to UW and its fabulous grounds.

Moody, Fred. *Seattle and the Demons of Ambition: From Boom to Bust in the Number One City of the Future*. New York: St. Martin's Griffin, 2003. A look back at Seattle's cravings to become world-class, from its pioneer days to the dot-com era.

Ochsner, Jeffrey Karl, ed. *Shaping Seattle Architecture: A Historical Guide to the Architects*, 2nd ed. Seattle: University of Washington Press, 2014. The people behind Seattle's greatest structures.

Shorett, Alice, and Murray Morgan. *Soul of the City: The Pike Place Public Market*. Seattle: The Market Foundation with University of Washington Press, 2018. Update of a 1982 history of Seattle's favorite shopping/tourist experience.

Westerlind, Linnea. *Discovering Seattle's Parks: A Local's Guide*. Seattle: Mountaineers Books, 2017. Exploring famous outdoor magnets and hidden gems.

Williams, David, Jennifer Ott, and HistoryLink staff. *Waterway: The Story of Seattle's Locks and Ship Canal*. Seattle: HistoryLink/Documentary Media, 2017. How a project to improve shipping and industry reshaped Seattle.

Williams, David B. *Too High and Too Steep: Reshaping Seattle's Topography*. Seattle: University of Washington Press, 2017. Early Seattle's regrades, landfills, and rerouted waterways.

Woodbridge, Sally B., and Roger Montgomery. *A Guide to Architecture in Washington State*. Seattle: University of Washington Press, 1980. The many strains of late-19th- and 20th-century design, as applied to the built environment.

Websites

Arcade, arcadenw.org. A sounding board for the Northwest design community.

Crosscut, crosscut.com. An inside-the-sausage-factory look at how Seattle politics and civic planning really work.

Feet First, feetfirst.org. Volunteer group promoting walkable communities.

HistoryLink, historylink.org. An ever-growing online encyclopedia of Seattle and Northwest history.

Seattle Architecture Foundation, seattlearchitecture.org. Tours and educational programs about the city's past and its future.

Seattle Bars, seattlebars.org. One man's quest to visit every existing Seattle bar (now up to 1,556, including ones that closed after he got there).

Seattle Walk Report, instagram.com/seattlewalkreport. Anonymous comic panels about cool things seen on our streets.

Index

About the Author

Clark Humphrey has seen Seattle transform from a boom-and-bust industrial city into today's fast-growing, fast-moving tech mecca. His other books include *Loser: The Real Seattle Music Story* (reissued by MISCmedia), as well as *Vanishing Seattle* and *Seattle's Belltown* (both by Arcadia Publishing). He writes daily about the city, its growth, and its contradictions at miscmedia.com.